Managing Organisational Politics

How coaches and mentors can help

*David Clutterbuck, Lise Lewis, Tim Bright
and Riddhika Khoosal*

Open University Press

Open University Press
McGraw Hill
Unit 4, Foundation Park
Roxborough Way
Maidenhead
SL6 3UD

email: emea_uk_ireland@mheducation.com
world wide web: www.openup.co.uk

First edition published 2023

A catalogue record of this book is available from the British Library

ISBN-13: 9780335249473
ISBN-10: 0335249477
eISBN: 9780335249480

Library of Congress Cataloging-in-Publication Data
CIP data applied for

Typeset by Transforma Pvt. Ltd., Chennai, India

Managing Organisational Politics

Praise page

"*Understanding organisational politics is critical for coaches who want to bring a systemic lens to their work, as all decisions and relationships involve the management and exercise of power. This fascinating title brings this topic to life, blending insight and practice on diverse themes from gender to digital and from presence to psychological safety.*"

Prof Jonathan Passmore, Professor of Coaching & Behavioural Change, Henley Business School, UK

"*This book is an invaluable guide for anyone seeking to create an inclusive work environment despite the complexities of office politics. Drawing on real-world experience, the authors offer insights on how to use mentoring and coaching for individuals willing to create an environment where we can feel "be-longing", while also understanding the dynamics of organizational politics. Whether you're a seasoned executive or just starting your career, I believe this book is a must-read for anyone seeking to thrive in today's competitive business environment.*"

Dr Riza Kadilar, EMCC Global President, The Netherlands

Contents

About the authors

David Clutterbuck is one of the last active pioneers of coaching. Author of more than 75 books, he is visiting professor of coaching and mentoring at four universities. David co-founded the European Coaching and Mentoring Council (EMCC), for which he is a roving Special Ambassador. He is Practice Lead for Coaching and Mentoring International, a global network of coaching and mentoring trainers and practitioners.

Tim Bright works internationally as a coach and consultant. He is based in Istanbul with OneWorld Consulting and, as well as doing executive coaching, he designs and supports mentoring programmes and works with leadership teams. Tim often works with leaders taking on new roles. He is a co-founder of EMCC Turkey. And he has written 74 fewer books than David!

Lise Lewis is an executive coach and award-winning coach supervisor with an international practice. She is a designer and provider of accredited coach and supervisor training for individuals and corporates through Bluesky International. Immediate Past President of EMCC Global and currently Special Ambassador, she has written 74 and soon to be 73 fewer books than David!

Riddhika Khoosal works internationally as an organisation development consultant, facilitator, speaker and executive coach. In her professional career of over 15 years, she has worked for blue-chip organisations such as Unilever and Johnson & Johnson. Currently, she works with leaders and teams from around the globe to help them thrive in this world of increasing demand. She too has written 74 fewer books than David!

Acknowledgements

Thanks and appreciation to all those who contributed data informing the chapters:

- Everyone who agreed to be interviewed and provide case studies, whose confidentiality is respected.
- Everyone who completed the survey questionnaires.
- Andy Preston, Mayor of Middlesbrough.
- Philippe Rosinski, author of *Coaching Across Cultures*.

Introduction

A fascination with politics and the assumptions people make about politics is one of several threads that have brought the four of us together. Each of us has experienced politics in a wide range of contexts, both inside the workplace and out.

For David, engagement with politics began 45 years ago, when dissatisfaction with perceived corruption and failure to listen to residents' needs stimulated an involvement with local politics. An invitation to become a candidate for Parliament led him to interview serving politicians from all three main parties at the Palace of Westminster – and to decide that that wasn't the way he wanted to have an influence on the world! Decades of working with Boards in many sectors and countries illuminated the many ways in which politics (with a small 'p') paralleled politics with a big 'P' – and also some of the differences. Among the many influences on his thinking about politics have been the novels of C.P. Snow, on academic politics, Barry Oshrey's insightful *Seeing Systems*, which explores the political culture of top, middle and bottom, Machiavelli, and political satire, as expressed most eloquently in the TV series *Yes, Minister*.

As a coach supervisor, the systemic nature of organisational politics is an everyday factor in the complex dilemmas that coaches bring to him for analysis. This book is an opportunity to reflect on that complexity, in ways that will help both coaches and their clients bring about positive change.

For Lise, politics first featured in her career when becoming aware of politics specifically relating to gender. She noticed that when women were judged on appearance rather than merit, being young and attractive gained the reward of recognition while mature women became invisible. The 'glass ceiling' – which still exists in less-enlightened organisations – meant women were banging their metaphorical head a few rungs from the top of the promotion ladder. Meetings meant competing for voices to be heard, assumptions made for being a note-taker and coffee-maker, and ideas being snatched from mid-air.

Leading a team as president of a global organisation expanded her horizon of politics when joining a culturally rich community of mentors, coaches and supervisors. Cultural norms, socialisation and inherent bias equal a diversity of expectations for meeting personal agendas. Political practices are wide-ranging and encourage agile attention to gain the positive outcomes that healthy political activity achieves. Thirty years of working as a coach and supervisor have significantly extended Lise's understanding of how the workplace continues to evolve, how the value of coaching supports the leadership journey and the timeliness of this book.

For Tim, an interest in organisational politics developed out of his coaching practice. As discussed in Chapter 2, he noticed common issues that were limiting the success of the executives he was working with and realised that a lot of these connected to organisational politics. In discussion with supervisors and other coaches and mentors, Tim noticed that many professionals in the coaching and human resources industry are themselves very uncomfortable with organisational politics and the use of power, and often have a negative view of the whole subject, which limits their ability to support their clients.

Over a number of years, Tim developed the view that politics is itself neutral and that we need to develop political astuteness to be successful. Coaches and mentors have an important role to play here and he hopes that this book will go some way in encouraging and supporting coaches and mentors as they work with their clients in this challenging, fascinating and important area.

For Riddhika, her interest in organisational politics was sparked early in her corporate career after experiencing first-hand the costs of being politically naïve. Following a series of hard lessons, she reluctantly conceded that if she were to succeed in her career, she needed to engage. For many years, she held a negative view of workplace politics, straddling the tension between 'playing politics' and remaining authentic and in line with her values.

Riddhika's view of workplace politics changed, however, in the latter part of her career. The 'aha' moment for Riddhika was recognising that workplace politics was itself neutral – that when leveraged skilfully and with integrity, it can engage networks of power and influence for the greater good of all. It is her hope that this book helps leaders and coaches develop their knowledge and skills so that the predominant experience of workplace politics shifts from negative to positive.

One of our first challenges was to place boundaries around what we would cover. We chose not to encompass coaching in the context of 'big P' governmental politics, on the grounds that it is a very different phenomenon – not least because there are so many differences between voters and organisational stakeholders. That's a book in itself! But we did talk with professional politicians and have included some of their perspectives in our frameworks and models. We are particularly grateful for the insights from Andy Preston, who is currently Mayor of Middlesbrough and who mentions using 'emotional intelligence in understanding how people who hear the message need to know the context – particularly if it's a difficult message that's conveyed'.

We want to call attention to the language we use when discussing politics at work. The terms we use often indicate our attitude to the subject. We know that books or articles that talk about 'office politics' probably have a negative view of these activities. Similarly, when we hear about 'corporate politics'. And we know that nobody likes 'political games'. However, if we talk about 'effective use of influence' or 'managing our impact', then we are probably talking more positively. We have chosen to use the term 'organisational politics' in this book as we see it as more neutral. As we discuss in Chapters 2 and 4, we believe that political activities can be positive or negative, and we judge people's political behaviours in terms of their intentions, goals and outcomes. We encourage all readers to reflect on their own terminology, as a shift in the words we use can open up different ways of thinking and engaging.

In writing this book, we wanted to do more than collate existing concepts and materials. So we undertook our own research into workplace politics, which we reveal in Chapter 1. We also developed our own instrument to stimulate reflection by coaches and their clients around political competencies and political intelligence. This is presented in Chapter 10.

The bulk of the book explores major themes both from the literature and from our own research. First, we look in Chapter 2 at the concept of political astuteness and high integrity politics. Then in Chapter 3, we place politics in the wider context of culture. Chapter 4 looks at how political power is misused in organisations and Chapter 5 digs deeper into organisational culture with a review of the role of psychological safety (or the lack thereof).

Chapter 6 builds on the cultural aspects of organisational politics through the lens of gender. It reveals how the hidden politics of gender disempower women in the workplace and suggests some of the remedies, which may be applied through coaching.

Chapter 7 takes us into reputation building and networking, introducing the concept of *authentic reputation management*. Chapter 8 develops another context – the role of technology in organisational politics. In 'big P' politics, technology has been increasingly used to sway electorates. Our focus, however, is more on the micro-influences within teams and groups resulting from how technology is used.

Chapter 9 pulls together many of these themes within the context of the workplace of tomorrow to discuss the changes needed in leadership behaviour to achieve positive political environments and the role of coaches in supporting these shifts.

And in Chapter 10 we offer a tool which can help everybody reflect on their own attitudes to politics and their political astuteness. We believe this can be helpful in many coaching and mentoring engagements.

While we have offered some practical advice, our primary objective in putting together this book has been to stimulate conversations between coaches and between coaches and their clients on how to rehabilitate organisational politics into the beneficial skillsets and behaviours we believe it should exemplify.

In short, we want to encourage coaches, mentors and their clients to make conversations about organisational politics overt, positive and valued. And in doing so, to create working places where people can truly thrive!

David, Lise, Tim and Riddhika

1 Survey research findings

Riddhika Khoosal

This chapter explores the key themes that emerged from our research and distils some of the key insights and questions that require further exploration. While we do not claim to have all the answers, we hope our findings will move us further along in our quest to stamp out the negative side of workplace politics and enable the positive.

The research

The purpose of the research was to explore and gather the experience of leaders, coaches, mentors and supervisors on the range of issues they consider to be 'political', how they view the challenges in working with organisational politics and practical approaches for maintaining integrity. In order to achieve this, each respective audience was invited to partake in the research by completing an audience-tailored online questionnaire-based survey that was shared on social media platforms and by various coaching bodies via their mailing list.

Once the survey results were obtained, an analysis of the data was performed to better understand the trend of responses. The survey was completed by 116 leaders, 113 coaches and mentors, and 47 supervisors from a variety of locations across the Americas, Europe, the Middle East and Asia-Pacific regions.

A view on politics

When it comes to corporate politics, almost everyone has a story to tell. What we weren't prepared for in our research, however, was that most of the stories would be negative. Especially given 72% of our survey respondents reported viewing politics as neither good nor bad (depending on motivations and how it is put into practice). As we delved further into the data, we uncovered a plausible explanation.

The neutral perspective was skewed towards the view held by coaches, mentors and supervisors. Leaders, on the other hand, were more inclined to view office politics as 'to be avoided at all costs' or a 'necessary evil'. Given that leaders are on the frontline and are having to deal with the full spectrum of office politics on a day-to-day basis, this discovery was less surprising.

What was unifying among all three groups surveyed was a view that executives having 'political astuteness' (being politically aware and able to work with different power relationships and conflicting objectives) was important, with over 90% viewing it as 'very important' or 'quite important' in the workplace.

When asked how often each group encountered politics in their respective roles, over 70% reported 'all the time' or 'frequently'.

Bringing these findings together, it became evident that workplace politics is a prevalent part of corporate life and that being able to navigate it effectively is imperative if we are to succeed in our endeavours. What also became clear is that a gap exists between this intellectual understanding and the lived experience of many as they wrestle with how to develop the necessary skills to navigate workplace politics competently.

Defining workplace politics

We began by asking, 'How would you define politics in the workplace in one or two sentences?'. The answers were surprisingly consistent across five themes:

It's always present

Workplace politics can be likened to 'air'. It's always present and a vital part of the corporate ecosystem. It can also be clean, polluted or extremely polluted. It's the unspoken or implicit 'rules' of the organisational culture. It's the methods by which people make decisions and relate to one another. Simply put, it's how things get done in reality. Avoiding it is as futile as avoiding air. It is essential to our survival and understanding politics plays an important role in deciphering the health of an organisation.

It's a display of power dynamics

Office politics can be viewed as 'power in play' and refers to the covert and overt use of power to attain objectives. We've all had to deal with it in one form or another. The boss's pet. Turf wars. Rank and privilege. Being excluded from conversations. Not being consulted on key decisions. Whether we like it or not, navigating power games is an inevitable and inescapable aspect of workplace politics.

It's a way to influence outcomes

This aspect of workplace politics involves knowing who to talk to, how to talk to them and when, to get the results you want and which you think are in the interests of the organisation. It acknowledges that your work alone won't get you promoted and that relationships are integral to success. It's understanding the relational environment in which you work and how best to leverage it to achieve results. In taking the time to understand different perspectives and work towards alignment, we develop rapport and win support.

It's a way to advance self-interests

This widely understood aspect of workplace politics is what gives it a bad name. Often because these self-serving instincts are accompanied by poor judgement and toxic behaviours. This includes withholding or manipulating information to gain the upper hand, using networks to gain status, abusing rank or privilege, and being seen to do the right thing instead of doing the right thing. All in the spirit of advancing one's own agenda over the greater good of the organisation and of other stakeholders.

It's used in service of self-preservation

The ongoing calculation of whether we feel comfortable speaking up and risking our safety or staying silent in the name of self-preservation plays a central role in corporate politics. It can weigh on every decision we make as we continuously assess the best way forward. And if we deem the risk too high, we default to the path of least resistance, which can at times be in direct opposition with our authenticity and values. We bend to the egos of colleagues, make decisions to assuage the feelings of others and suppress our views to stay 'onside'. All in the interest of self-preservation.

A negative perspective can be formed quite quickly, especially when people are perceived to be putting their own agenda before that of the organisation and when they feel at times the need to compromise their values in the interest of safety. There is, however, a positive side to workplace politics that frequently gets overlooked – something we'll explore in more detail in the following chapters.

Politics exists on a spectrum

A knife can be used to chop vegetables that feed an entire village or used to stab someone in the back. How we choose to engage with it determines if it becomes a tool for good or bad. Workplace politics is no different.

The bad side

The self-serving characteristic of corporate politics cannot be ignored. When sifting through the data, countless responses were describing corporate politics as the deliberate behaviours of people enacted to influence or manipulate others to advance themselves. Whether it be to land their next promotion or simply survive the next restructure, office politics is notorious for satisfying one's own agenda and creating a toxic work environment.

To further understand the adversities faced, we asked leaders and coaches what some of the most negative impacts of office politics are on people and organisations. What our findings confirmed is that ultimately no-one gains from the bad side of politics. Neither the people involved nor the organisation.

Fear promotes silence. Innovation and collaboration are stifled. Trust is eroded. Engagement and motivation plummet. Injustice and discrimination divide. Authenticity and ethics are threatened. Mental health and self-confidence take a hit. Performance suffers. And the bottom line is, good people leave.

The negative impacts of workplace politics revealed in our research are shown in Table 1.1.

Table 1.1 Negative impacts of workplace politics

Impacts	Details
Loss of talent	• Good people leave – thus often leaving behind those who are complicit and accepting of the status quo
Disengaged workforce	• A withdraw of discretionary effort • Low engagement and motivation leading to frustration and poor performance
Performance suffers	• Time spent on managing politics rather than delivering outcomes • Poor decision-making, increased stress, lack of focus and an inefficient allocation of resources • As good people leave, expertise and historical knowledge leave with them
Good people don't progress	• 'Good people' without political skills don't get promoted to senior levels. Often due to holding a fixed negative view that politics equates to 'manipulative scheming' and thus do not develop the necessary skills, resulting in missed opportunities
Toxic behaviours	• Gossiping, blaming, lying, secrecy, irritability, being judge-mental, bad manners, unprofessional communication, insincerity, various us-them constructs, bullying, avoidable rivalries and evasiveness
Harms organisational culture	• Reputational damage making it hard to keep and retain talent, i.e. 'That organisation does some good stuff but inside it has a toxic work environment'
Feeling devalued	• A 'blindness' to the potential of individuals. Being cast aside, being marginalised and side-lined • Feeling that playing the field is unfair, because politics is informal and behind the scenes and so those who under-stand and engage have access that others do not

Table 1.1 (*continued*)

Impacts	Details
Career-limiting if you don't engage	• Fear of losing job, derailing career, side-lining, poor career development, loss of promotion, loss of stakeholder support, inability to integrate successfully into new role or team
Fear of speaking up	• Not speaking up due to fear of damage to career and reputation • If you say anything against the idea of the group, then you'll lose favour • Not sharing thoughts openly, leading to gossip and decisions being made behind closed doors
Pressure to conform	• An inability to be true to oneself, placing the needs of more powerful people first • Connecting to the 'right people', being nice, saying what is expected
Mental health/ burnout	• Sadness, illness, sick leave, stress, anxiety, mental wellness challenges created by toxic culture • Deep distress – people not coping with backbiting, backstabbing and other toxic behaviours • People burn themselves out rather than maintain healthy boundaries out of fear of repercussion
Lack of self-confidence	• Loss of personal and professional confidence • Damaged sense of self • Imposter syndrome • Fear of failure or of not being good enough
Innovation is stifled	• Lack of trust and therefore of willingness to offer up ideas. Holding back, thus stifling collaboration and innovation • Reduced speed, agility and flexibility in the organisation • Groupthink phenomenon • Inhibited creativity and shared responsibility
Discrimination	• High levels of political activity without good cultural 'hygiene' can and does lead to a sense that the organisation rewards those who play the game best, not those who work hardest to achieve organisational goals • Lack of meritocracy • Unfit managers appointed for political considerations
Loss of trust	• Distrust and hostility among employees, loss of confidence and trust in leaders, loss of belief that the organisation is doing the 'right thing' • Feeling that values and procedures are not respected or upheld
Ethics	• Confusion about what is right or wrong as political behaviour can 'market' attitudes and influence people

(*continued*)

Table 1.1 (*continued*)

Impacts	Details
Lack of diversity, equality and inclusion	• Politics means that for those outside of/excluded from the 'game', it is hard to be heard or to influence • Loss of the opportunity of teamwork and the contribution that diversity could bring • Meetings happening over breakfast or golf outing, thus excluding those who are not part of the clique • Females finding it hard to be heard or to influence in a male-dominated environment

The good side

When engaging in the good side of office politics, we build alliances and influence outcomes without devaluing others or neglecting the interests of the organisation. We dream courageously and collaborate willingly. When power and influence are used in this way, office politics serves as a positive and igniting force for learning, growth and innovation.

To explore the beneficial aspects further, we asked leaders and coaches what some of the most positive impacts of office politics are on people and the organisation. What was abundantly clear in their responses is that leadership plays a critical role in creating the conditions for the good side of workplace politics to prevail. When leaders role-model positive, inclusive political behaviours, they encourage transparency, respond constructively, weed out toxicity, build trust, invite safety, advance communication, promote collegiality, foster learning, fuel innovation and build consensus for change. In short, they cultivate the relational dynamics that bring out the best in people and drive business performance.

The positive impacts of workplace politics identified in our research are shown in Table 1.2.

Table 1.2 Positive impacts of workplace politics

Impacts	Details
Values-based leadership	• Stamp out negative political games by calling them out rather than simply navigating the status quo • Set the right culture for a learning environment • Role-model positive, inclusive political behaviour that encourages professionalism, builds trust, enables a positive working environment, empowers others, promotes collegiality • Recognise and weed out toxicity

Table 1.2 (continued)

Impacts	Details
Strategic leadership	• Transparent about political systems in operation • Can successfully navigate political situations honourably to achieve results • Understand the importance of communication, alliances and transparency, and utilise these effectively • Can 'reflect and respond' as opposed to 'react or withdraw' • Shield team members from difficult stakeholders • Overt individual and team development on how to manage politics
Better decision-making	• Positively motivated to exert one's influence for better decision-making • More robust decision-making due to more collaborative relationships
Develop better relationships	• Invest the time to engage effectively with stakeholders • Develop partnerships and alliances • Balance cohesion and challenge • Don't take things too personally and respond constructively
Engagement and wellness	• Foster a cooperative and productive environment • Build an atmosphere of transparency and recognition • Reduce anxiety • Build connection and inner motivation • Empower teams and individuals • Greater diversity and inclusivity • Support talent development
Enabling dissenting opinions to be heard and valued/courage to speak up	• Develop a climate of trust and psychological safety • Value vulnerability as a courageous act and not a weakness • Embrace diversity of views • Exposure to a wide range of perspectives and experiences • Strong team cohesion • People feel empowered to raise issues or ask questions
Thinking outside the box/innovative solutions	• Able to leverage an organisation's full competency set • Break silos • Robust debate allows more creativity and experimentation

(continued)

Table 1.2 (*continued*)

Impacts	Details
Building consensus for change	• Understand the different agendas of others • Able to anticipate conflict and contention • Able to have difficult conversations while protecting own brand and move the conversation forward • Enable co-creation by tapping into collective wisdom
Being able to address the 'elephant in the room' (what many notice but no-one mentions)	• See the institutional/organisational tensions and opportunities and help the business to address them
Open discussion of conflict on values	• Open, respectful dialogue between different levels in the organisation

Typical political challenges in the workplace

You can't escape politics, no matter which organisation you work in. Avoiding it is career-limiting and engaging with it can be challenging. This reality was underlined in our research findings as collective political challenges came to the fore. Delving deeper into the analysis, four key themes emerged that helped us to understand these challenges further: information flow, power dynamics, conflicting agendas and lack of fair treatment. As we work through each theme respectively, we'd like to acknowledge that the examples shared are merely the tip of an enormous iceberg of challenges that stem from office politics. Let's dive in.

Information flow

Our analysis yielded three key findings when it came to the flow of information in the workplace. First, employees withhold what they know and hoard information. Second, the access to information gets blocked by power dynamics and a lack of transparency. Third, people are selective in the information they share to advance their own agenda.

The sharing of information

Sharing information is widely encouraged within organisations as it leads to greater creativity, innovation and performance. Yet, many employees withhold what they know and hoard important and useful information, creating an issue for those who depend on that information. As such, the latter end up turning to political manoeuvring to obtain what is needed.

The access to information

Transparent leaders keep their team in the loop, share information freely and invite open communication with the team and its stakeholders. Unfortunately, not all leaders are transparent. Some restrict the flow of information and stifle communication, creating political challenges for their team. A common example of this is team members having to go through the chain of command instead of speaking directly with other senior leaders, creating inefficiencies.

Being selective with information

There is much to be gained from being open about team failures. Exploring what hasn't worked creates a forum for feedback, learning, improvement and innovation. Yet, putting a positive face on even when things aren't going so well is common practice. The fear of unfavourable consequences drives many employees to sugar-coat or manipulate information to 'keep stakeholders happy' and influence agendas that are detrimental to business performance.

Power dynamics

Power and influence are central to workplace politics and often central to workplace challenges. Our findings revealed how power dynamics and influence have a bearing on how decisions are made, how willing people are to speak openly and how people gain advantages within the workplace.

How decisions are made

Decision-making is a critical component to the functioning and success of any team or business. But the decision-making process isn't always easy or straightforward. Despite academic research showing that diversity leads to better decision-making, our findings reveal that many people still struggle with being included in the process. Hierarchical power and influence are still deciding factors as to whether or not you get a seat at the decision-making table. The impact of this closed approach is that employees who have value to bring, yet are excluded, feel disempowered and disengaged. And both the individual and organisation lose out.

Also revealed was the role that corridor conversations play in influencing the outcome of decisions, outside of the forum created to make decisions. Unsurprisingly, engaging in backdoor channels is a hallmark of office politics and is often seen to create an unfair playing field in the workplace.

Our findings also disclosed a tendency for leaders to base their decisions on the furthering of their own agenda rather than operating in the best interest of the organisation. In such instances, leaders can be seen to:

- not give resources to team members they don't get along with
- operate with a lack of transparency and suppress the involvement of their subordinates

- not 'let go' of areas of decision-making that could be absorbed by the team
- make ego-based decisions related to dominance and assertion of control, rather than expert knowledge
- choose to save face instead of admit mistakes.

Feeling unable to speak openly

Creating the conditions in which employees feel safe to speak openly, have candid conversations and raise issues is imperative to succeeding in today's world. When the right conditions are not present, however, it's in our human nature to 'play it safe' by holding back and staying silent. The tendency to not say what you think and to avoid speaking truth to power out of the fear of negative repercussions is a common political challenge faced in the workplace.

When safety is at risk, people are inclined to:

- agree with their boss, even if it's not reflective of how they feel
- suppress their own view to fit in with the accepted one
- not openly communicate when there are problems or cover up mistakes
- let their boss take the credit for their work
- dance around leaders' opinions and preferences for the sake of being liked.

How relationships are leveraged

Developing strong relationships and gaining influence are fundamental to achieving one's goals in the workplace. Overlay this with our innate human need to be liked and feel safe and it's no surprise that various power dynamics emerge in the workplace, such as cliques, coalitions and preferential treatment. When these power dynamics are self-serving, political challenges arise. In such cases, those who are not astute could be influenced in a potentially unethical or harmful manner.

Instances in which relationships are leveraged for self-gain include:

- People being appointed because of their political affiliation rather than merit
- People having 'the ear' of superiors and gaining an unfair advantage
- The formation of cliques or 'inner circles', creating an uneven playing field
- Colleagues receiving favouritism and operating 'above the law', despite their performance being suboptimal
- Fostering relationships in service of blatant career climbing.

Conflicting agendas

In an ideal world, when faced with the choice, leaders choose the interests of the organisation ahead of their own. What our research confirmed, however, is that we don't live in an ideal world. Copious responses pointed to people engaging in workplace politics for self-advancement to the detriment of the organisation. It also indicated that, when confronted with conflicting agendas, people tend to bat for themselves, whether it be between leader to subordinate, peer to peer or department to department.

Examples of conflicting agendas include:

- Not promoting a high-performing team member due to the workload that would be created for the leader to replace them
- Basing decisions on political considerations rather than acting on expert advice
- Infighting over the allocation of resources
- Turf wars between departments
- Having to manage due to lack of insight at the top of what's happening on the ground.

Lack of fair treatment

Politics exists on a spectrum, and the degree to which you need to contend with it is largely shaped by the environment in which you work. The line manager you report to, the team you belong to, the department you work in and the organisation you work for, all contribute to your day-to-day reality. In some environments, things happen in an atmosphere of trust and respect with the good side of workplace politics being the dominant cadence. In others, conflict and fear are the bedrock from which hierarchy, rank and privilege are not only important, but feel like a matter of survival. In such environments, toxic behaviours arise, typically leading to blaming, shaming, discrimination, favouritism and inequality.

When the environment is toxic, challenges include:

- Leaders rewarding those who 'play the game' best, not those who work hardest to achieve organisational goals
- Being passed over for a promotion
- Lack of trust and thus an unwillingness to offer up ideas
- Credit theft by colleagues
- Ethical dilemmas
- Needing to 'sell a line' and not be transparent with certain stakeholders
- Having to follow a directive that is in direct opposition with your values
- Not being rewarded fairly
- Not feeling valued
- Side-lining or removing subordinates that raise concerns
- Lack of opportunity or support.

Table 1.3 summarises the typical political challenges faced in the workplace.

Table 1.3 Typical political challenges in the workplace

Information flow	*The sharing of information* • Hoarding of important and useful information *The access to information* • Stakeholders influencing decisions outside of the forum created to make decisions • Not being connected to key people or conversations • Leaders blocking the flow of information *Being selective with information* • Putting a positive face on even when things aren't going so well • Storylines being manipulated to create a specific view
Power dynamics	*How decisions are made* • Leaders not giving resources to team members they don't get along with • Leaders operating with a lack of transparency and suppressing the involvement of their subordinates • Leaders not 'letting go' of areas of decision-making that could be absorbed by the team • Leaders making ego-based decisions related to dominance and assertion of control, rather than expert knowledge • Leaders choosing to save face instead of admitting mistakes • Decisions having to be approved by the top • Leaders 'pulling rank' *How relationships are leveraged* • People being appointed because of their political affiliation rather than merit • People having 'the ear' of superiors and gaining an unfair advantage • The formation of cliques or 'inner circles', creating an uneven playing field • Colleagues receiving favouritism and operating 'above the law', despite their performance being suboptimal • Fostering relationships in service of blatant career climbing *Feeling unable to speak openly* • Agreeing with your boss even if it's not reflective of how you feel • Suppressing your view to fit in with the accepted one • Not openly communicating when there are problems or covering up mistakes • Giving your boss credit for your work • Dancing around leaders' opinions and preferences

Table 1.3 (*continued*)

Conflicting agendas	*Hidden agendas for self-gain over organisational interests* • Not promoting a high-performing team member due to the workload that would be created for the leader to replace them • Basing decisions on political considerations rather than acting on expert advice • Infighting over the allocation of resources • Turf wars between departments • Having to manage due to lack of insight at the top of what's happening on the ground
Lack of fair treatment	*Toxic environments* • Leaders rewarding those who 'play the game' best, not those who work hardest to achieve organisational goals • Being passed over for a promotion • Lack of trust and thus an unwillingness to offer up ideas • Credit theft by colleagues • Ethical dilemmas • Needing to 'sell a line' and not be transparent with certain stakeholders • Having to follow a directive that is in direct opposition with your values • Not being rewarded fairly • Not feeling valued • Side-lining or removing subordinates that raise concerns • Lack of opportunity or support

Biggest political challenges facing leaders

Having excavated the landscape of typical political challenges faced by leaders, we also wanted to understand what they felt were the biggest political challenges. Putting the question forward in a multiple-choice format, here's what we learned.

Just over 60% of leaders found 'Identifying the key influencers and their motivations' and 'Aligning organisational and personal values' the most challenging. Half the respondents identified with 'Taking a balanced view of politics'. And less than half selected 'Building support for your goals' and 'Confidence building' (see Figure 1.1).

Of those that selected 'other', responses included:

• Providing motivating and aspirational opportunities for all (diversity and inclusion)

• Top management being able to identify that often the challenges lie at the top with them, and thus taking necessary corrective action

- Encouraging the right behaviours that build trust and openness
- Educating on how to be politically savvy.

Figure 1.1 Leaders' response to the question, 'What in your opinion are the biggest challenges for leaders in managing organisational politics?'

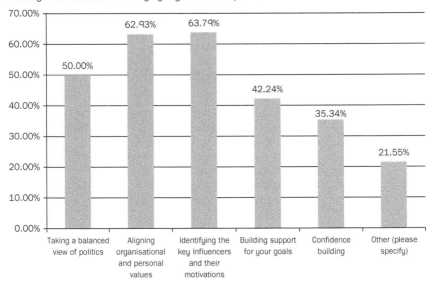

What these findings underscore is that to overcome the challenges of today, organisations need to refocus their efforts on creating a climate of transparency and trust whereby people feel supported at work and connected by a shared purpose.

Remaining authentic in the face of overly political behaviour

A common challenge when faced with overly political behaviour is having to wrestle with the choices that support our ideals and at the same time preserve our safety. Political dilemmas arise when the two are at odds – when we feel forced to compromise our ideals out of self-preservation or leave the organisation to keep our values intact.

So, how do leaders adapt to their environment without jeopardising their own values? To understand this challenge further, we asked leaders how they remain authentic in the face of overly political behaviour by others.

The following strategies were uncovered in our research:

- Talk about the facts and leave emotions out
- Take a timeout to reflect, then respond
- Stay true to core values at all costs
- Stay curious and engage in open dialogue
- Promote transparency and sincerity
- Call out unacceptable behaviour
- Stay focused on the goal
- Perform regular self-reflection
- Attract the right talent.

Further detail on ways to remain authentic in the face of overly political behaviour revealed in our research is shown in Table 1.4.

Table 1.4 Ways to remain authentic in the face of overly political behaviour

Behaviour	Details
Talk about facts and leave emotions out	• Stay focused on facts, data, numbers • Take emotion out of the discussion • Keep the vision of the company at the forefront • Stay calm and composed • Seek commonality and build on this
Take a timeout to reflect, then respond	• Take time to think things through • Engage in conversation away from the heat of the moment
Stay true to core values at all costs	• Regularly check-in on values and personal motivations • Remain true to core values, which sometimes means losing or rejecting opportunities • Role-model having discussion and debates in the appropriate forums, even if it means facing up to uncomfortable truths
Stay curious and engage in open dialogue	• Openly share views and create the environment for team to do the same • Invite diverse opinions to discussions • Put yourself in the other person's shoes to better understand motivations and behaviours
Promote transparency and sincerity	• Encourage a daring culture of feedback that supports transparency • Have the courage to express opinion or decisions that may be unfavourable

(continued)

Table 1.4 (*continued*)

Behaviour	Details
Call out unacceptable behaviour	• Call out inappropriate behaviour and show vulnerability • Take a direct approach, challenge appropriately, discuss and moderate • Seek to understand the motivations and diagnose how the system may be incentivising those behaviours • Ask skilful questions to help unearth motivations • Voice opinions by highlighting openly but diplomatically feelings of being uncomfortable in raising an issue
Stay focused on goal	• Focus on the business goal • Reinforce the importance of focusing on needs of the people/the organisation/clients/customers
Perform regular self-reflection	• Engage in regular self-reflection and self-awareness • Coaching and mentoring • Focus on the growth opportunity
Attract the right talent	• Recruit the right talent to uphold the cultural values

How coaches describe political environments in organisations

When asking coaches to describe the political environments in organisations they experience as a coach, their responses were consistent with our overall findings – it varies greatly. Some can be toxic and harmful while others can be transparent and supportive.

What also remained consistent with our research was the negative aspects of workplace politics overshadowing the positive, and the surfacing of the aforementioned themes: information flow, power dynamics, conflicting agendas and lack of fair treatment.

The descriptions of political environments in organisations shared by coaches included:

- Biases are present
- Do not reward fairly
- Fear-based culture
- Cloaked conflicts of interest
- A culture based on winning
- Power plays are routine
- Information gets concealed

- Toxic behaviours are prevalent
- Not everyone is politically astute.

Further detail on the descriptions shared by coaches of political environments in organisations is shown in Table 1.5.

Table 1.5 Summary of how coaches responded to the question, 'How would you describe the political environments in organisations you experience as a coach?'

Theme	Description	Details
Lack of fair treatment	Biases are present	• Environments in which clients are challenged with gender, cultural and language biases
Lack of fair treatment	Do not reward fairly	• Increased workload without adequate compensation (title, remuneration or feedback) • Infrequent professional development or performance reviews • Environments where relationships matter more than results
Power dynamics	Fear-based culture	• Clients unwilling to have open and straight conversations owing to the fear of adverse consequences. This often results in senior management being fed with what they want to hear not what is actually happening • Authoritarian – communicating what is 'expected' as right or wrong can manifest as coercion of people, behaviours, actions • Full of red tape • Lack of transparency • Narcissistic behaviour widely demonstrated • Environment built around self-survival • Low level of trust
Conflict of interest	Cloaked conflicts of interest	• Managing appearances • Clash of egos • When personal ambition creates blinkers for senior people, obscuring judgement
Power dynamics	A culture based on winning	• Decisions based on one winning and one losing
Power dynamics	Power plays are routine	• Silos of power – held by isolated groups • Operating in one's own self-interest • Us against them mentality • Say the right things rather than do the right things • Power is achieved through relationships

(continued)

Table 1.5 (*continued*)

Theme	Description	Details
Information flow	Information gets concealed	• Hidden agendas – manoeuvres are well hidden or covered up
Lack of fair treatment	Toxic behaviours are prevalent	• Integrity not part of leadership principles • Aggressive and harmful behaviour • Lack of respect of boundaries or ethical behaviour • Organisation espouses values but the politics outweigh them
Power dynamics	Not everyone is politically astute	• Clients can be naive to it, not really noticing or understanding the impacts • Frustration about needing to 'play the politics' and feeling repulsed doing it

What alerts coaches and mentors to political challenges faced by clients

Coaches and mentors can play a vital role in developing their clients' skills of working within a political environment, while maintaining their own integrity. In particular, helping them develop their political awareness (understanding how the systems work) with political astuteness (knowing when and how to exert influence).

To better understand how coaches and mentors support their clients, we asked them: 'What alerts you to the political aspects of the issue that clients bring to coaching?'. The following indicators were shared:

• A lack of clarity
• Have trouble explaining decisions
• Talk about leaders and colleagues
• Express challenges regarding career progression
• Talk of playing the game
• A lack of commitment to the organisation
• Behaviours or outcomes that defy logic
• A perceived lack of influence
• Reference to unwritten rules
• Share differing perspectives
• Don't feel free to speak up
• Convey differing agendas
• Feel stuck or powerless
• Face a clash in values
• Talk of developing alliances.

Further detail on what alerts coaches and mentors to political challenges faced by clients is shown in Table 1.6.

Table 1.6 Summary of what alerts coaches and mentors to political challenges faced by clients

Impacts	Details
Show a lack of clarity	• Lack of clarity of what's going on in the organisation
Trouble explaining decisions	• Difficulty explaining or justifying decisions taken by others • Stated reasons for particular action do not appear genuine, reasonable or clear • Business decision is taken without regard to hard facts
Talk about leaders and colleagues	• Lots of talk about bosses and top managers • How they talk about others in the organisation; the vocabulary and strength of feeling expressed • Negative comments about competing colleagues • Talk of individuals 'getting their way' • Coachees' comparisons of themselves and others • Stress, blame, fear and focus on others rather than the task • Needing to provide context on the wider system
Express challenges regarding career progression	• Talk of people movements and the impact that has on them and/or their team • Conversations about navigating the informal reward system • Sharing they need something upwards, outwards or sideways that touches their work or career objectives • Expressing frustration about their inability to progress (career development not supported or expectations not being met) • Perceived subjectivity on performance evaluations • Not feeling appreciated or heard • No discussion about personal aspirations and goals to meet company's vision despite efforts made
Talk of playing the game	• When clients express they 'Can't keep up the game' and feel they are often one step behind co-workers who use strategies to get ahead • Trying to make meaning of what happened in a situation (details of who benefited from an unusual course of action) • Clients might ignore obvious solutions because of the perception that it would be unacceptable by key players • Expressing fear, self-doubt, lack of confidence and concern over how to create change or exert influence • Discussions on cliques or groups that exclude others • Perceptions of bias or unfair treatment

(continued)

Table 1.6 (*continued*)

Impacts	Details
A lack of commitment to the organisation	• Client places self-interest over organisational interests • Actions that are rooted in insecurity and personal gain rather than team wins
Behaviours or outcomes that defy logic	• When a direction is not followed despite logical arguments (often other factors at play) • Seemingly illogical obstacles or blockages • Perception of hidden agendas
A perceived lack of influence	• Talk of lack of access to 'informal' networks • A struggle to influence others • Behaviours which show that there is a division in how people are treated and perceived • Feeling inadequate or afraid of engaging in politics • Don't feel understood or heard
Reference unwritten rules	• The 'we don't go there' unspoken behaviour as to how issues are (or are not) addressed • The level of awareness the client has of the written and unwritten rules and what consideration they have given them in the issue they are dealing with
Share differing perspectives	• When clients talk about 'their perspective' or 'their view', or discuss how different people see a topic from different perspectives • Conflicts or differences of opinion that they're having to deal with
Don't feel free to speak up	• Degree of freedom in expressing opinions when discussing management issues • Reluctance to comment on colleagues • Any discrepancies between views they express and their own values • Difficulty in speaking up to those higher up in the organisational hierarchy • Discomfort in voicing views honestly and openly to people at work, especially to certain individuals or groups with power • Not feeling comfortable to contribute in meetings
Convey differing agendas	• Conflict between colleagues (same team and different teams) • Conflict between managers and their staff • Issues around decision-making and resource allocation

Table 1.6 (*continued*)

Impacts	Details
Feel stuck or powerless	• Using expressions like 'we have to do that', 'that's the way it is here', 'we have no choice', 'they insist on it'. • Feeling the inevitability of an outcome • Tolerating destructive behaviours in the workplace • Having to make decisions they don't agree with • Sense of hopelessness and not being able to change or influence the system
Face a clash in values	• Incongruence between work requirements and their deeply held values
Talk of developing alliances	• Talk of needing to form alliances (an important factor to get things done) • Women working in male-dominated environments feeling the need to fit in to a 'macho' culture

Effective ways coaches, mentors and supervisors can support clients through organisational politics

An effective coach, mentor or supervisor supports their clients or mentees to reflect deeply and question their assumptions. In doing so, they help them to identify learning opportunities, grow their understanding of themselves and the world around them, and take steps to achieve change.

Practical tools and approaches that coaches, mentors and supervisors can use when helping clients or mentees develop their political awareness include:

• Helping them understand the complexities that surround their political issue. This could include identifying key influencers and their motivations.

• Asking questions that help to expand their understanding of their own thinking processes and to recognise that there are alternatives. For example, 'What would be the benefit of taking a different perspective on this?'

• Helping them articulate their values and reflect on what's most important so they can take a resonant course of action.

• Working on developing the skills and resources to handle political issues. For example, helping them see patterns in the interactions they have with key colleagues: do conversations and situations keep repeating themselves?

• Helping them grow from negative political encounters. Useful questions might include: 'What can you learn from this experience?', 'What other choices do you have in how you choose to interpret this experience?'

- Helping them be authentic in their responses to political issues. For instance, helping them prepare conversations, which will enable them to talk with colleagues at a values level – sharing what is important to each other.
- Helping them take a systemic view on politics. A simple technique could be to ask the coachee to take the perspective of another player in the issue, or to think through who else might see it radically differently and then ask for their input.
- Helping them build alliances by identifying what they could do to support each of their key colleagues and seek opportunities to do so frequently.
- Help build their confidence and support for their goals. For instance, rehearsing difficult conversations with them so they are better equipped.

Collectively, these interventions can transform how the coachee/mentee engages with workplace politics and result in more favourable outcomes.

Conclusion

Our survey showed that organisational politics is important to people and although many people perceive politics as a neutral activity, their own experience of organisational politics is mostly negative. Coaches, mentors and leaders agree that developing political astuteness is an important skill that should be worked on in coaching engagements. We will explore these issues and possibilities in the remainder of this book.

2 Political astuteness

Tim Bright

In the early 2000s, I noticed that two coaching clients I was working with were using very similar language to describe their frustrations at work. They were both in their mid-thirties and were identified as successful, high-potential current and future leaders for the large multinational companies they worked for. And they were both complaining about the same thing.

> *There's too much politics here.*
>
> *I'm focused on results not relationships.*
>
> *Some people here talk too much and get promoted because they are nice to the right people.*
>
> *I refuse to go to art events that our company sponsors; people only go to brown-nose our boss.*
>
> *The company should recognise what I'm doing and manage/promote me accordingly.*

And their bosses and Human Resources (HR) colleagues who gave us input for the coaching assignments were telling them both the same things. They needed to build better relationships and alliances across the organisation, use a range of influencing skills and not conflict directly with so many people.

Because I was coaching these two individuals at the same time, and their words seemed to echo each other, I started thinking a lot more about this. These two executives were great examples of Marshall Goldsmith's maxim of 'What got you here won't get you there.' Their direct, task-oriented working styles, using buckets of intelligence and hard work, had led to a series of promotions and marked them out as high potential leaders. However, their lack of organisational political skills was threatening to derail their careers. And it wasn't just a lack of skills. When I asked them how they might engage across the organisation and build better relationships with peers and other stakeholders, they replied that they actively didn't want to do this: 'I don't want to kiss ass just to get on' and 'I don't want to be fake, or pretend to be someone I'm not' were their responses.

Both these executives exhibited common, black-and-white views of organisational politics. They were task-oriented and believed they should be 100% authentic all the time. They perceived anything else as fake and did not want to spend any time on activities that were not directly related to their business goals.

After reflecting on these cases and discussing them in supervision and through dialogue together with the individuals and their stakeholders, I realised that these executives needed two things: first, to be persuaded to see organisational politics differently, in a way that would help them flourish; and, second, to develop, practise and use the skills of positive organisational politics. In other words, they needed to become more politically astute.

Since then, political awareness and astuteness are something I've been interested in as a coach and have observed it as an important issue with many clients. I don't think that this is just a case of noticing something more when you are aware of it. I believe that developing political awareness and astuteness is an important development need for many people working in organisations, and I think it is something that coaches often do not pay enough attention to.

In the survey that we carried out as part of the research for this book, 90% of participants told us that political astuteness is quite important or very important. So what is political astuteness? Is it a good thing, and can we develop it in ourselves and others? These are the questions for this chapter.

As we have seen in Chapter 1, the definition of organisational politics is, in itself, political. There isn't one straightforward definition that satisfies us all. For the purposes of this chapter, I'll think of organisational politics as 'the informal use of power', using Egan's (1994) definition. I believe that to be successful we need to embrace and engage with the ideas of power and influence in organisations. If we engage reluctantly, thinking 'I wish I didn't have to do this, but I must', then we are unlikely to achieve our goals.

Political astuteness – what is it?

I believe that 'political astuteness' is a good term for what we all need to develop. We can also talk about political 'skill' or 'savvy'.

The most helpful conceptualisation of political astuteness comes from the research work of Jean Hartley and her colleagues. They 'constructed and tested a framework of political astuteness skills, which sought to broaden the concept beyond the narrow account of "political skills as self-interest" that is present in much management literature' (Hartley et al., 2013).

Before we look into their framework, let us briefly consider what we mean by 'astuteness'. Dictionary definitions of astuteness vary. The Cambridge English dictionary talks of 'the quality of being able to quickly understand a situation and see how to get an advantage from it'. The Collins COBUILD Dictionary says astute people 'show an understanding of behaviour and situations, and are skilful at using this knowledge to their own advantage'. Some definitions have a negative tone, referring to being 'crafty', 'wily' or looking for your own advantage. Others, such as Princeton's WordNet, are more positive, seeing astuteness as 'marked by practical, hard-headed intelligence'.

Jean Hartley (2015) uses different definitions of political astuteness, which sometimes also include this ambiguity, talking of 'understanding the lay of the land and using it to your advantage' and 'the art of getting things done'. I agree with the view she has expressed that 'political astuteness is about working with contest and conflict to achieve organisational and social goals'.

Rather than seeing political astuteness as inherently a good or bad thing, based on my experience of working with executives, I believe it is most helpful to see political astuteness as neutral. As with other competencies, such as persuasion or negotiation skills, political astuteness can be used for good or bad ends. If we perceive political astuteness as negative, we are unlikely to engage in the power dynamics that will allow us to achieve our goals. If we see it as purely positive, we are at risk of overlooking the dangers for ourselves and the organisation that political behaviours can bring.

We judge the ethics of someone's political astuteness by their intentions and the outcomes of their actions. Imagine you are working in a large multinational organisation and you interview a candidate at 4pm on a Friday afternoon. You decide you want to recruit them, but they have another job offer they will accept on Tuesday, unless you can get an offer to them on Monday. In most large organisations, it's impossible to make a formal job offer so quickly. However, you may use your informal power in the organisation to get the offer made on Monday. You might persuade HR to require fewer interviews than usual and to do reference checks more quickly. You could persuade other colleagues to interview the candidate over the weekend. If your use of political skills and influence in the organisation to get the candidate recruited is because you think they are going to be good for the organisation, this is positive. However, if you are using political skills in order simply to get a friend of yours recruited because they'll be loyal to you, this is negative politics.

If we are going to achieve our organisational and social goals, we need to engage positively with informal power and influence and develop our own political astuteness.

Hartley (2015) has created a valuable framework of political astuteness skills, organised into five categories: personal skills, interpersonal skills, reading people and situations, building alignment and alliances, and strategic direction and scanning.

Personal skills include self-awareness, self-control and being proactive in terms of managing relationships and agendas.

Interpersonal skills are listening effectively, encouraging others to be open with you, being curious and making others feel valued.

Reading people and situations encompasses understanding others' perspectives – their values, motives, interests and goals. Also, understanding organisational power structures and the threat that you may present to others.

Building alignment and alliances is about understanding who you can work with to achieve organisational goals. Making alliances and knowing when to collaborate or compete.

Strategic direction and scanning involve understanding the right time to move quickly on your agenda and when to hold off. Having a clear sense of purpose and picking up signals from colleagues and external sources on what is changing in your environment and what is coming next.

Research by Gerald Ferris and his colleagues (2005, 2007) identifies four dimensions of political skill: social astuteness, interpersonal influence, networking ability and apparent sincerity.

There is a great deal of similarity between the classifications of Hartley and Ferris. One difference that stands out is the importance that Ferris places on apparent sincerity. This may be considered under Hartley's personal skills; certainly being perceived as sincere is important in helping us to achieve our goals. Hartley also adds strategic direction and scanning, which capture an important competency. This ability to maintain a clear sense of purpose and also to understand how to work effectively in changing circumstances is necessary to achieve aims with political integrity. Successful high-integrity political actors have a strong sense of timing and know when to act, which is based on this sense of direction and scanning.

In my experience, I find Hartley's classification most helpful and I use this actively with my own coaching clients. Because we focus on high-integrity political astuteness, we believe this involves being sincere, not just appearing to be sincere. We understand sincerity as meaning being aware of and congruent with our emotions and saying what we genuinely feel and believe. This also connects to having a clear 'sense of purpose', one of the elements of Hartley's 'strategic direction'.

Both these models are based on *skills*. We also believe that political astuteness includes *beliefs*. To be effective politically, we must believe in the importance of political engagement. As in the examples at the start of this chapter, some people don't want to engage with issues of power and influence and believe that they should be judged simply on their results. To be politically astute, we must first see political engagement as worthwhile. We need to see it as appropriate to build networks and alliances and to plan how we will achieve our goals in the context in which we are operating.

Ideally, we should believe in *high-integrity politics*. By this we mean that we can and should proactively engage with networks of power and influence, while acting in line with both our own values and for the good of our organisation and the world around us. Acting in line with our own values means that we don't support ideas we don't believe in or pretend to be something we are not. We don't pretend to like golf just to get on well with our boss. Also, it means acting in line with the interests of the organisation, not just our personal interests. High-integrity politics involves promoting ourselves, but it doesn't involve putting others down.

We see true political astuteness as a combination of the skills outlined by Hartley, and an effective mindset that involves being sincere and believing in the importance of engaging positively with power and influence. We can therefore define high-integrity political astuteness as:

> *That set of beliefs and skills that enables us to act sincerely in line with our values and for the good of our organisation and the wider world to effectively achieve our goals in a complex environment of conflict and contest.*

How can we help others, or ourselves, to develop political astuteness?

We see political astuteness as a set of beliefs and skills that can be developed. We will look at how a coach, mentor or colleague can help others. You can also apply these ideas to yourself. As coaches or as colleagues, we need to help people in different ways – we need to discuss the mindset around politics, and also raise awareness of which behaviours people already use well and support the development of new behaviours.

First, we need to work on the level of *beliefs*. Take a moment to reflect on your own, or your colleagues', beliefs about power and politics.

Research by Casciaro, Gino and Kouchaki (2014) shows that professional networking makes some people feel dirty. We have heard many coaching clients describe networking or political activities at work as 'bullshit' or 'the way poor performers get ahead'. If this is how you think about organisational politics, then you won't engage effectively. This is a type of self-limiting belief and it's appropriate for us to challenge coachees' or colleagues' thinking on this and raise their awareness of different ways of looking at the situation. However, we can challenge these beliefs in a number of ways.

One way is to use a cognitive behavioural approach to consider the pros and cons of our current beliefs. We may quickly realise that these negative beliefs about politics get us few benefits (except perhaps propping up our egos or giving us excuses for limited success) while leading to many disadvantages – not building connections, missing out on opportunities for learning or gaining information, losing visibility within the organisation.

In my coaching, I have noticed that many people who don't want to engage politically have a strong belief in the 'power of ideas', as Brandon and Seldman (2004) describe it. They believe that in an organisation the best idea should win, irrespective of influence and relationships. I've found it useful to challenge this view by discussing how we are all forced to make decisions with limited time and information and that often, having influence works. I ask clients who manage a team, 'imagine that tomorrow you are given the opportunity to send just one of your team on a valuable and prestigious training programme, and you need to decide quickly who to send. What would you actually do?' Although the ideal approach might be to consider every team member, look at their development plans and think carefully about who has received what training investments already, we rarely work like that. In most cases, a team leader will quickly decide on a person and extend the offer to them. It is likely that person is someone who has proactively engaged with the team leader, built a relationship with them and demonstrated their interest in further development.

They have probably used political astuteness to have a positive impact on the team leader and it has worked.

Once we realise that we all apply short-cuts when we make decisions, and we tend to give more attention and resources to those who actively put themselves in front of us, it becomes clearer that we need to do the same with our bosses and other stakeholders. We all have to make decisions quickly and with limited resources. We don't have time for the 'power of ideas' to win in every case. The quality of your ideas – and your performance of course – matters, but if you don't present them to other people, you and your ideas may not get noticed. This doesn't mean that your bosses are stupid or badly intentioned, simply that they don't have the time to fully research every decision they make.

Another approach that can be helpful is to look at other people in the organisation and analyse their approach. I often hear coaching clients say, 'I don't want to be like John, he's so political.' Here I find Brandon and Seldman's 'organisational savvy continuum' very useful.

At one end of the continuum we have 'over-political' and at the other 'under-political' (Figure 2.1). Over-political people are those who use organisational politics too much and expect to do well purely on the basis of their relationships or ability to influence. Under-political people are those who refuse to engage in the dynamics of power and influence, and simply think that their work and ideas should be recognised for what they are.

Brandon and Seldman also characterise this as the power of ideas versus the power of person. Let's consider the extremes of each view. The believer in the power of ideas thinks that results and ideas should always speak for themselves, and decisions are based on meritocracy and open agendas. They believe we should have power based on the substance of our ideas and always do the right thing. The believer in the power of person, in contrast, believes in the power of a position or role rather than the power of ideas. They focus on image and perception and believe in doing what works and maintaining private agendas when necessary. They expect decisions to be based on relationships and believe in the importance of self-promotion.

An important point is that these views are at opposite ends of the political savvy continuum. In reality, we are all at different points along this continuum. We can say to our clients or colleagues, 'Okay, you don't want to be like John; don't be, he's over-political. But where are you on this organisational savvy continuum?' People often immediately recognise that they are under-political, and we can then ask what would it be like to move a few steps towards the middle and become 'appropriately political'.

Figure 2.1 Brandon and Seldman's 'organisational savvy continuum'.

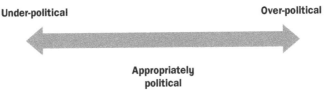

Under-political   **Over-political**

**Appropriately
political**

For the executives that I mentioned at the beginning of this chapter, this approach was what made the difference for them and enabled them to develop more effective political skills. Realising that they didn't have to be like those over-political people they didn't respect and that they could find an alternative, politically appropriate way to act in ways that didn't compromise their integrity, opened up new and more effective ways of thinking and acting for them. Gerard Egan (1994) suggests similarly that being politically naive and politically cynical are at opposite ends of a spectrum and that again we need to be somewhere in the middle.

We define 'appropriately political' as using high-integrity political skills to achieve goals that are in line with your values and are good for your organisation as well. You are not just pushing your own personal agenda.

We can also argue that being appropriately political is our duty. If you have good ideas and can help your organisation to achieve its goals, then it's your duty to make sure that you have that impact. If you stand aside and let less effective people take centre-stage or get promoted instead of you, then you are doing your organisation a disservice. I have used this approach with coaching clients, asking 'do you honestly think you will do a better job of this than Peter?' If 'yes', then you owe it to the organisation to take this responsibility and it is your duty to use high-integrity political skills to get this role.

High-integrity politics includes a sense of *stewardship* for the organisation (Egan, 1994). As an employee, you use your power and influence for what is best for the long-term interests of the organisation. You have the choice to do this working by yourself, or by building a coalition with others, or by finding ways to help the system challenge itself.

How can we help others build political astuteness using Hartley's framework?

Hartley and her colleagues have researched how people develop their political astuteness. In a UK survey of 1,500 people (Hartley, 2015), the following were the most common ways people said they developed their political skills:

* 88% learnt from their mistakes
* 86% gained on-the-job experience
* 85% learnt from handling a crisis
* 77% followed the good example of a senior manager
* 70% learnt through observing bad behaviour from a senior manager.

Hardly anyone said that they had developed their political astuteness through training courses, and when they had, these were negotiation courses. Hartley comments that 'Experience, either good or bad, has been identified as the best source for developing this vital leadership skill.'

Coaching and mentoring can play an important role in filling this need. Encouraging people to reflect more on their experience, and using coaching tools to help people develop their political astuteness, can make a significant contribution.

We can and should work on political skills in coaching. Coaches and mentors can help their clients think about the wider systems at work and the interactions between different players and engage with the complexity around them. We can also use these approaches on ourselves or with our colleagues. Hartley's political astuteness framework gives us an excellent guide to working on these issues, so let's work through it category by category.

Starting with *personal skills*, we need to raise awareness of self and others. This is where our coaching questions and our quality of attention and listening skills are invaluable. Simply getting people to focus on the idea of power dynamics can be very helpful. We can ask people what the current dynamics are, where do power and influence lie, how do they act at the moment? Where do they lie on the organisation savvy continuum, are they under-political or over-political, and where do they want to be? Encouraging people to take a proactive approach is essential here too, so they are setting the agenda rather than just responding to events or the actions of others.

Like self-awareness, self-control is something we need to develop in ourselves and others. Many of the tools of emotional intelligence and emotional agility recommended by authors such as Daniel Goleman and Susan David are valuable here. In particular, the method of labelling our emotions, naming them specifically, and remembering that 'you are not your feelings' is helpful. As Susan David suggests in *Emotional Agility* (2016), rather than saying 'I'm anxious' or 'I'm stressed', saying 'I am feeling anxious' or 'I notice I'm feeling stressed' begins to create critical space between us and our emotion. If we can treat our emotions as valuable data sources about what is important to us, this is a huge step towards effective self-control. To be politically effective, we need self-awareness and self-control.

In terms of *interpersonal skills*, emphasising the importance of listening, and helping our clients and colleagues develop that muscle, is important. Engaging positively with others and encouraging openness is difficult for some people, often because of bad experiences they have had in the past. Encouraging them to be open with others and make a first move towards trust is often helpful and later in this chapter I will offer some justifications for this approach.

Curiosity is undervalued by many and developing a genuine curiosity with people can really help in terms of building awareness and relationships. Reminding clients of the benefits of curiosity and seeing it as a valuable characteristic is helpful.

Reading people and situations is also a skill that we can work on in ourselves and with our colleagues and clients. Some people routinely think about what other people's perspectives may be and what their values, motives and interests are. Others don't. I've asked clients, 'what do you think the reasons might be for this person's actions?', only to receive the answer 'how should I know?' or shallow answers based on no reflection. We need to help people think more about what the perspectives of others are and to imagine how the situation looks from where other people are sitting. Over time, people can build this habit and it becomes easier for them to think about this.

Asking people 'what threat might you be seen as posing to others in the organisation?' can open up avenues to explore. Many executives see themselves as victims of power structures without realising the actual or perceived threat they represent to others. I have asked, 'What do you think person X would say about what is going on here, or the role you are playing?' If I get the answer that person X won't be honest, I sometimes ask: 'Imagine that we give person X a truth drug, so they have to be honest with us. What would they say then?' Or, if I want to be less dramatic, 'How do you think person X might feel about what is going on here, or the role you are playing?'

Based on insights gained from these questions and encouraging people to see themselves as players within the political dynamic, we can explore with them what alternative tactics and strategies might look like and how they can ethically reach their own goals.

Encouraging clients to map out networks of power and influence in the organisation is another useful strategy. We can draw such networks, or even use items to build a tabletop constellation of who holds what power within the organisation. When we do this, we often find that clients leave out certain people and doing this exercise can prompt them to think more broadly and beyond the obvious players. Asking who has influence, who has power, who has information and who can access resources, all are useful questions. Mapping out the motivations of different people within the system is also helpful.

Encouraging clients to actively think about *building alignment and alliances*, and building high levels of trust with others in their organisation, can also break down potential victimhood and suggest actions to take. Identifying existing alliances in the organisation can help us plan activities as well. If you are unable to directly access someone who has power in an area that is important to you, perhaps you can build a relationship with someone who can then influence them on your behalf.

Hartley's final category, *strategic direction and scanning*, is often overlooked. We should encourage clients to step back and think about what their purpose is and what important goals they really want to achieve by using power and influence. We can also encourage people to look out for signals within and beyond the organisation about what is important and what is changing in the world in which they operate. And finally, focusing on timing is important. As well as discussing what actions to take, in situations related to power and influence, choosing when to act is vital.

Insisting on a certain decision being taken when the organisation is focused on something else probably isn't going to work. Understanding when your successes have increased your influence and authority and that now is a good time to push for something that you want to achieve, is an important part of political astuteness. Also understanding the financial situation across the organisation can guide us on when to ask for extra resources and when not to. Some executives I have coached have an almost instinctive sense of when to act to achieve difficult organisational goals. Others don't pay attention to the time dimension in the organisation and simply make proposals or push for changes when they want to.

As coaches and mentors, we can help people in this area simply by drawing attention to the time dimension. Useful questions include: 'When would be the best time to take action or present this idea?' and 'What are the benefits or risks of delaying this action?' In my experience, focusing on the idea that there will never be a perfect time when everything is aligned can help us be more aware of the risks of delay and encourage appropriate action.

Other activities we can use with coachees or colleagues

Working with a coachee to analyse their use of *political capital* can also be effective. It can be helpful to think in terms of a bank account that you make deposits into and withdrawals from. The executive can think about how much political capital or power is in their account now, and how that compares with others. They can then think about what activities will earn more political capital and what actions will mean them spending some of their political capital. This is particularly important for newly appointed managers. For example, if you want to change most of your team, you may have the political capital to do so, but if it doesn't work out well you may well find that you don't have the capital left to do other things that you need to do.

I often work with executives who think they are starting from zero, and need to win political capital. They tend to underestimate the political capital they already have. If you are new in a role, you have been recruited or promoted because of what you have done before and what you offer to the organisation, and there is a positive belief that you can do this job well. So you are not starting out with zero political capital. Rather than looking for 'quick wins', I encourage people to think about what political capital they already have, and what they want to spend this on, as well as what they can do to earn more political capital.

Working with coachees to *plan positive political activities* is also useful. For coachees who resist the term 'political', one can talk of 'influence and impact' instead. For example: 'How do you want to engage with informal power in your organisation?', or 'How do you need to influence different stakeholders to reach your goals?'

Thinking about how coachees can build a more effective network is important. If appropriate, we encourage them to consider strengthening that network now, so that it is available to them when they need it in the future. (See Chapter 7 on social presence and networking for more on this.)

Coaches can also work with executives to help them develop persuasion and influencing skills, and to consider how to make proposals attractive to others. Experts such as Robert Cialdini, in his book *Influence* (2007), share valuable insights that we can all benefit from. Developing storytelling and presentation skills is also a valuable focus.

When clients find themselves challenged by organisational politics, coaches and mentors can work with them to rehearse critical conversations that they need to have. It can also be useful to reverse roles and get the client to take the role of the person they will be having a challenging conversation with.

I also ask people I work with to consider the institutional resources they can use to win support for their goals. The coach or mentor can help them to identify blind spots, or unexploited strengths and connections they may have, and encourage and challenge them to take action.

Political skill is often a kind of intuition. Egan talks of good managers having 'a third ear and a third eye. In observing and listening to the workplace, they see the below-the-surface dynamics of their companies and departments' (1994: 57). In my coaching work, I have noticed that some managers are much more tuned into and aware of political and power issues than others. Like a muscle, this kind of skill can be developed. We all have this ability to sense the unwritten rules and hidden activities to some degree, but by becoming more aware of this sense we can enhance it and use it more effectively. As coaches and colleagues, we can encourage others to focus on their intuition, listen to it and develop it by paying attention to it. We can ask questions to draw clients' attention to the political dynamics of a system and ask them what they might not be noticing.

We do have to be careful though, to ensure that our intuitions are not just reflecting outdated views or inappropriate prejudices. Bringing our intuitions to awareness in dialogue and examining them with a trusted colleague, coach or mentor are valuable. By doing so, we can determine whether our intuitions are helping us understand a situation more effectively, or are reinforcing unhelpful prejudices. In this way, we can help develop our political intuitions and skills over time.

Are we dreaming?

We have offered our definition of high-integrity political astuteness as:

> That set of beliefs and skills that enable us to act sincerely in line with our values and for the good of our organisation and the wider world to effectively achieve our goals in a complex environment of conflict and contest.

One reaction to this might be that we are being impossibly idealistic. In seeing the positive benefits of political astuteness, are we moving too far away from most people's lived experience? We saw in the results of our survey that for most people their experience of politics is negative. Is it possible to act both in line with our own values and for the good of our organisation and the wider world?

First, we should mention that political astuteness is not only about dealing with conflict but also about creating sufficient agreement to work more productively as an organisation. Individuals and organisations are increasingly involved in many different forms of working partnerships, and relationships within organisations are also changing to include many ways of working beyond a traditional employer and employee structure. A move to more flexible working is accelerating these changes. As organisations change their internal structures more quickly, and complex, matrix and agile structures become more common, the informal use of power, as opposed to formal structural power, is becoming increasingly important. In this context, political astuteness is a set of essential skills and beliefs that are needed to mobilise organisations and align diverse people around goals and initiatives.

In situations of conflict, there are also reasons to believe in the power of positive political approaches. Research done in the field of evolutionary biology suggests that organisms that cooperate with others, rather than simply competing, tend to flourish. Computer simulation models built using elements of game theory based on the Prisoner's Dilemma and, critically, using repeated rounds of the game, show that organisms that have a default approach of cooperating with a stranger until learning from experience not to cooperate with a particular individual, succeed in multiplying the most successfully. In his book *The Evolution of Cooperation* (2006), Robert Axelrod demonstrates that trusting first and then responding in whatever way others respond to you is the most successful tactic for flourishing. He summarises the lessons learned from these experiments as:

- *Be nice*: cooperate, never be the first to attack.
- *Be provocable*: return attack for attack, cooperation for cooperation.
- *Don't be envious*: focus on maximising your own 'score', as opposed to ensuring your score is higher than that of your partner.
- *Don't be too clever*: or, don't try to be tricky.

We see many examples of these lessons in our work and believe that in terms of organisational politics, we are most successful if we start from a position of trusting others and continue to act in that way unless someone demonstrates that they are untrustworthy, in which case we need to protect ourselves. Most of organisational life is built on repeated interactions and ongoing relationships, so this iterative model applies well to our daily experience.

The biologist Richard Dawkins (1987) builds on Axelrod's research and argues that contrary to Hobbesian views of nature as selfish, in fact 'nice guys finish first'. Living organisms engage in 'reciprocal altruism'. And 'many wild animals and plants are engaged in ceaseless games of the Prisoner's Dilemma, played out in evolutionary time' (Dawkins, 1989: 203). We can learn from these natural models as they give support to the idea that the most effective strategy is to trust others first and then respond in line with whatever way they act towards us.

Adam Grant reaches similar conclusions in his more recent research for *Give and Take* (2013a). Success in life is often attributed to talent, hard work and luck. Grant adds a fourth factor to this list – our reciprocity, the way we interact with others when exchanging value. Grant argues that people tend to operate as what he calls 'takers, matchers, or givers'. Takers strive to get as much as possible from others, matchers aim to trade evenly, while givers are the rare people who contribute without expecting anything in return. Most people are matchers. Matchers and takers rank in the middle in terms of success in most professions. The people who achieve the most (and the least) success are givers. We also explore these ideas in the context of networking in Chapter 7.

According to Grant's research, being a successful giver comes with many benefits. Giving forms more robust relationships, increased happiness and better performance at work. There's just one problem – research also shows that while some givers thrive at work, others burn out.

Successful givers are what Grant calls 'smart givers' and he says they distinguish giving from being timid, available and empathetic. Successful smart givers value the greater good, while *also* valuing their own needs and interests. They're both altruistic and ambitious. By paying attention to their own self-care, they avoid 'generosity burnout'. Selfless givers might be more generous, in principle, because they always put other people's interests ahead of their own. However, Grant's work suggests that selfless givers are actually less generous in the long run, because they eventually run out of energy for giving.

Grant argues that smart givers are more successful because they build bigger and deeper networks. They collaborate more effectively. To become more of a giver, he recommends that we look for '5-minute favours' we can do for others.

In terms of cooperating with others, echoing Axelrod's research, Grant recommends us to start by giving and to observe others, and if they are acting selfishly, we should switch from giving to matching. Note that we don't need to become takers; we switch to matching, only helping the taker if they help us, or others, in return.

How do we identify the takers? In Grant's survey, up to 19% of people were rated as takers. Sometimes it's obvious, but Grant has these recommendations to recognise those takers who are hard to spot, or 'fakers' as he calls them. Takers typically promote themselves eagerly. They use words such as 'I' and 'mine' rather than 'we' and 'ours'. They treat people below them differently; they kiss up, and they kick down. They tend to be uninterested in people they feel they can't benefit from, while flattering people they think can help them get ahead. Faker takers create an excellent impression until they get what they want. They are often takers because they don't trust others' intentions but there is a possibility of turning them into smart givers, if we can build the right culture and demonstrate good intentions. 'Part of the solution must involve targeting the takers in the organization – providing incentives for them to collaborate and establishing repercussions for refusing reasonable requests' (Grant, 2013b).

How to build an effective culture of cooperation

In our experience, organisations are mostly made up of people trying to do the right thing, and wanting to act in ethical and cooperative ways. However, that is clearly not always the case.

How can we act effectively in more challenging situations? Grant usefully recommends that the 'key is for employees to gain a more nuanced understanding of what generosity is and is not. Givers are better positioned to succeed when they distinguish generosity from three other attributes – timidity, availability, and empathy – that tend to travel with it' (Grant, 2013b).

Grant (2013b) highlights interesting research by Harvard professor Hannah Riley Bowles. Bowles asked nearly 200 executives to role-play a salary negotiation in pairs, based on the situation of an employee being promoted. The male 'employees' negotiated average salaries of $146,000, while the females got $141,000, or 3% less. The women were more inclined to be givers. But another group of women achieved an average salary of $167,000, 14% more than the men. This group were asked to act as the employee's advocate. 'When they saw themselves as agents representing the interests of others, being tough was completely consistent with their self-images as givers' (Grant, 2013b). Each was fulfilling her responsibility to another person who mattered to her.

Other studies have shown similar results and suggest that those who are uncomfortable with self-advocacy can overcome their *timidity* by shifting their frame of reference and advocate for others who share their interests to achieve goals that will satisfy them all. If your position isn't shared by others, then imagining how a sponsor might argue on your behalf can help you adopt a more powerful tone and arguments to help you get what you deserve. Or imagine a friend was in your situation, how would you act to protect their interests? Taking these alternative perspectives enables people to overcome their own timidity.

There is a risk that givers spend too much of their time and energy on giving, so they need to set limits on their *availability*, and focus their giving on where it will have most impact.

Grant argues that *empathy* is a third trap givers need to avoid. Empathy can make life harder for givers as they spend time doing favours they can't afford and may be manipulated by takers. Grant recommends we can avoid this risk by taking perspectives (trying to imagine what others are thinking and what their interests are) rather than using empathy. In a negotiation study led by the Columbia psychologist Adam Galinsky, 40% of the perspective takers reached an optimally balanced agreement, whereas only 17% of the empathisers and the subjects in the control group did (Galinsky et al., 2008). So, rather than building our empathy, we need to build our ability to understand others' perspectives and interests. To encourage perspective-taking, we can ask clients to gather information about a counterpart's interests and to make a list of their own interests as well.

Grant (2013b) argues that there are three benefits associated with teaching employees about the power of agency, boundaries on availability, and perspective-taking. First, it saves givers from being taken advantage of and makes them smart givers instead. Second, it enables people who fear the potential risks of giving to contribute more. And third, it builds a culture of generosity that attracts more givers to the organisations and is less attractive to takers. Grant also notes that organisations are most effective when people are more generous.

Dealing with difficult or unethical people

How should we deal with the takers in our organisations or people with bad intentions? Grant has three suggestions (McQuaid, 2017). First, look for the moments when they are less selfish. There may be areas where these takers do give generously or have enthusiasm to share and we can focus on these areas. Second, gently letting people know they have a reputation for selfishness can motivate them to make changes. Reputation-based feedback can be effective as people don't want to be known as a taker. Finally, being clear about expectations and holding people to account for their actions can be effective in confronting takers.

Mark Goulston (2013) offers great insights and practical advice on managing conversations with difficult people. He suggests that what makes them so difficult to deal with is not your fear of provoking them, but rather 'your fear that after you do that, they will react in such an appalling way that they will so provoke and upset you that it will unleash a deep rage inside you, that you are so uncomfortable with and is so out of sync with how you view yourself'.

He recommends that we adjust our expectations. We usually expect people to behave reasonably, and the shock that we feel when difficult people do not do so can take us aback and be quite upsetting. Goulston notes that difficult people may appear to be caring and cooperative, but this only lasts until they get what they want. We shouldn't be fooled into thinking that they have changed. He recommends that when we have identified a person as difficult or untrustworthy, we need to protect ourselves. We should expect them to act only in their own interests even when they appear to be kind and caring.

Goulston recommends that in such circumstances, we should always pause before responding. No matter what the difficult person says or does, make a practice of waiting several seconds or more before you reply. Stay calm and keep your emotional distance.

Goulston offers three responses we can make to nearly every type of difficult person:

1 'Huh?': This one word can stop difficult people in their tracks. It should be spoken in a mild, neutral tone of voice. This is for when a difficult person says something ridiculous but acts as if they are being reasonable. This answer shows that what they are saying doesn't make sense and that we aren't engaging with it.

2 'Do you really believe what you just said?': Again, using a calm, non-confrontational tone. This works when people are exaggerating to throw us off balance. They may not engage and may just withdraw, which is fine.

3 'I can see how this is good for you. Tell me how it's good for me': This is good for dealing with a difficult person's unreasonable demands. If the person doesn't engage or changes the subject, you can state: 'Since it's not clear how this is good for me, I'm going to have to say no.'

In some cases, we may just need to disengage from a difficult person. We might say, 'Sorry, I'm finding this exhausting, and I need to preserve my energy. If you can find a way to talk with me instead of at me, I'm willing. Until then, count me out.' Then walk away. Goulston suggests it is easier to walk away from difficult people like this once we give up the expectation that we'll ever reach a win-win solution with them.

When dealing with takers, Goulston recommends that we make a mental list of ways the taker could help us. The next time the taker asks for a favour we can say, 'Yes! And you can help me out by ...'. If the person hesitates, continue with 'I assume you don't mind doing a favour for me in return?' If we insist on a quid pro quo each time, the taker will soon realise we are unwilling to be compromised and give up on trying to take from us.

Although we believe in the power of positive political engagement, if you are in a situation where you can't both act with integrity and achieve your goals, then you need to protect yourself and, if you are able to, you should move somewhere else.

Summary

In summary, we see high-integrity political astuteness as:

That set of beliefs and skills that enable us to act sincerely in line with our values and for the good of our organisation and the wider world to effectively achieve our goals in a complex environment of conflict and contest.

We see this political astuteness as an important, neutral competency, and we judge someone's ethics by looking at their intentions and goals and the outcomes of their actions.

Hartley's framework of political astuteness competencies – personal skills, interpersonal skills, reading people and situations, building alignment and alliances, and strategic direction and scanning – provides an excellent guide to what we should be focusing on when we are developing our political astuteness.

It also helps to consider the risks of being over- or under-political, and to find a middle zone of being appropriately political, in which we proactively engage with power and influence in line with our values and our organisational goals. This may involve promoting ourselves, but does not include damaging or attacking others.

Research by Axelrod, Grant and others suggests that positive political engagement, trusting others first, and then reciprocating in the same way that they treat us lead to the best outcomes. These examples can help us convince others of the benefits of high-integrity politics. When dealing with habitual takers, or people who are untrustworthy or unethical, we need to protect ourselves and we have looked at ways of doing this.

We can all benefit from reflecting on our political astuteness and coaches, mentors and colleagues can help us develop this competence. We first need to adopt the right mindset and believe in the benefits and possibility of high-integrity politics. We then need to raise awareness of how we and others currently act. Finally, we need to work on developing our competencies of political astuteness and taking the right actions.

Developing and practising our high-integrity political astuteness can reduce our anxieties, increase our happiness, help us achieve our goals and make our organisations better places for everyone who works there.

For coaches, helping clients reflect on high-integrity political astuteness can be one of the most meaningful and valuable ways we contribute to their development.

References

Axelrod, R. (2006) *The Evolution of Cooperation*, revised edition. New York: Basic Books.

Brandon, R. and Seldman, M. (2004) *Survival of the Savvy: High-integrity political tactics for career and company success*. New York: Simon & Schuster.

Casciaro, T., Gino, F. and Kouchaki, M. (2014) The contaminating effects of building instrumental ties: How networking can make us feel dirty, *Administrative Science Quarterly*, 59 (4): 705–735.

Cialdini, R.B. (2007) *Influence: The psychology of persuasion*, revised edition; first Collins Business Essentials edition. New York: Collins.

David, S. (2016) *Emotional Agility: Get unstuck, embrace change, and thrive in work and life*. New York: Avery/Penguin Random House.

Dawkins, R. (1987) *Nice guys finish first* [video documentary]. Available at: http://nature-documentaries.org/1500/nice-guys-finish-first-richard-dawkins-1987/.

Dawkins, R. (1989) *The Selfish Gene*, second edition. Oxford: Oxford University Press.

Egan, G. (1994) *Working the Shadow Side*. San Francisco, CA: Jossey-Bass.

Ferris, G., Davidson, S. and Perrewé, P. (2005) *Political Skill at Work: Impact on work effectiveness*. Mountain View, CA: Davies-Black.

Ferris, G., Treadway, D., Perrewé, P., Brouer, R., Douglas, C. and Lux, S. (2007) Political skill in organizations, *Journal of Management*, 33 (3): 290–320.

Galinsky, A., Maddux, W., Gilin, D. and White, J. (2008) Why it pays to get inside the head of your opponent: The differential effects of perspective taking and empathy in negotiations, *Psychological Science*, 19 (4): 378–384.

Goulston, M. (2013) Who's holding you hostage? Mastering difficult conversations, part 1: Conversations with difficult people, *Smart Brief*, 29 August. Available at:

https://corp.smartbrief.com/original/2016/05/whos-holding-you-hostage-mastering-difficult-conversations-part-1.

Grant, A. (2013a) *Give and Take*. London: Penguin.

Grant, A. (2013b) In the company of givers and takers, *Harvard Business Review*, April. Available at: https://hbr.org/2013/04/in-the-company-of-givers-and-takers.

Hartley, J. (2015) *Political Astuteness: An essential skill in the workplace*. The Open University Business School. Available at: https://business-school.open.ac.uk/news/political-astuteness-essential-skill-workplace.

Hartley, J., Alford, J., Hughes, O. and Yates, S. (2013) *Leading with political astuteness – a white paper*. Open University Business School. Available at: https://www.bl.uk/britishlibrary/~/media/bl/global/business-and-management/pdfs/non-secure/l/e/a/leading-with-political-astuteness-a-study-of-public-managers-in-australia-new-zealand-and-the-united-kingdom.pdf.

McQuaid, M. (2017) How to deal with takers at work – an interview with Adam Grant, *Psychology Today*, 10 October. Available at: https://www.psychologytoday.com/gb/blog/functioning-flourishing/201710/how-deal-takers-work.

Politics and culture

Tim Bright

In Chapter 2, we looked at how a coach or mentor can support an individual client in steering an authentic path through the political system of an organisation by developing their own political astuteness. Here we look at the system itself.

A culture is best understood as the values, beliefs, assumptions and behaviours shared by a group. In this sense, any group has a culture – families, countries, companies, teams. And the same cultural dimensions can be applied to these groups. In this chapter, we look at how cultural elements impact on organisational politics and how coaches and mentors can help their clients manage effectively in this area.

Some of the most interesting research work in this area has been completed in the realm of national cultures. Here, I will use two frameworks from the field of national culture that can be applied to any kinds of cultural differences, not just national cultures. Geert Hofstede was a pioneering cultural researcher, whose work on cultural dimensions grew out of large-scale research carried out on many individuals in companies around the world. The dataset has been expanded and revalidated since his original work in the 1960s and 1970s (see Hofstede, 2001; Hofstede and Hofstede, 2010). Philippe Rosinski has developed a comprehensive Cultural Orientations Framework, which covers a very wide range of concepts and carefully describes each of them as a dimension, in non-judgemental terms (see Rosinski, 2003). Other experts in the national culture space include Erin Meyer and Fons Trompenaars.

There is also a wide literature on organisational culture dating from the 1960s to the present, including Ed Schein, Charles Handy and Charles Hampden-Turner. Our focus here is on culture in its broadest sense and how different cultural assumptions lead to different perceptions about what is politically acceptable and politically effective. What the theorists on national culture have in common is, first, that they see multiple dimensions that enable us to distinguish one shared cultural mindset from another. Second, they see that conflict and challenges often arise from misapprehension of the intentions and expectations between people having different cultural norms and assumptions. And third, they see that 'cultural intelligence' (awareness of one's own culture as well as those of others) is an essential skill for managers and leaders in a connected world.

We discuss in Chapter 7 how individuals working alone or with a coach/mentor can analyse the sources of power in the context in which they are working, and prepare a stakeholder map to help them decide how to act. Reflecting on culture provides another lens for us to think through, and in terms of planning effective and high-integrity political activities, we need to be aware of the cultures that we or our clients are working in.

All organisations have a culture, all organisations have power distributed in different ways, and because of organisational interdependencies we all need to work with others and build coalitions in order to achieve our goals. How we work with power, and how we engage with political issues, will be different depending on our own specific cultural context.

Thinking through your own or your client's situation in terms of cultural dimensions will help you co-create effective strategies. For coaches and mentors working with clients in organisations that they don't know well, being sensitive to culture is particularly important. Whether your client is working in a Californian technology start-up or a large Middle Eastern family-owned and -led conglomerate will have a huge impact on which political strategies and tactics will be effective. With the growth of remote working, coaches and mentors now often work with clients operating in very different national cultures from their own. This makes it even more important to carefully reflect on the cultural context together, to ensure the best approach is taken. When looking at an organisation's culture, we have to consider the national and local context, the impact of the sector that the company is working in, the stage of growth that the company is at, the current economic circumstances of the business, and the impact of individual leaders and managers within the organisation. All these factors can impact the organisation's culture and determine which high-integrity political strategies will be most effective.

When companies merge or are acquired, they often talk about creating a 'third culture' using the best of both organisations. Often, one of the legacy company cultures comes to dominate, although different subcultures may persist for some time in different parts of the new entity. For example, the commercial function might be dominated by leaders from company A while production is still driven by people from company B, each applying their own legacy culture norms. Navigating politically within a merged company environment requires even more care and the balances and norms can change quickly, particularly when a previously strong leader leaves the organisation during or soon after the merger process.

There is also the culture of a team, referred to as an idioculture. This is often linked to the individual culture of the team leader, whose authority may oblige others to conform to their expected norms.

As culture is a facet of organisations, we don't normally talk about an individual's culture. However, we can think about our own individual cultural preferences. What cultural norms are we most familiar with and which do we feel most comfortable with? When thinking about political strategies, this is important as we may well have to get out of our comfort zone. Both Rosinski's and Hofstede's frameworks can also be applied to individuals (Rosinski has a free self-assessment tool available) and this is a useful way of helping us think about our own cultural attitudes and preferences.

When I work with clients in this area, I often ask them to estimate where their own national culture sits on each of these dimensions, and then where do they sit as an individual? Interestingly, almost everybody describes their own dominant national cultural preferences and then says that they themselves are different from these norms. We all say this and it's true. We do differ from the norms of our own culture, even though they are statistically valid tendencies.

I find it helpful for clients to identify the cultures of their own company and also to think about the culture in different units. For example, what is our overall company culture? How does the culture differ from HQ to the company subsidiary in this country? How is it in Sales or Manufacturing? In what ways does the culture appear very similar across all areas and where is it different?

Although Hofstede and others provide solid data to compare national cultures, I don't find the specific numerical data so important. What is more valuable is raising people's awareness of the different dimensions in which we can think about culture. And to raise our client's awareness of their own culture as a culture. We all tend to think of ourselves as normal, and other cultures as varying compared to that baseline. Some cultures are more hierarchical, some less so, but we are normal. Once we realise that there is no normal, and see our own culture as a position on a set of dimensions, just like every other culture, we are well placed to work with culture effectively. Because we all have our own cultural preferences and norms, there is no objective position outside of culture from which we can observe other cultures.

All individuals are different, and yet there are valid tendencies that vary across cultures. As Florence Kluckhohn and Fred Strodtbeck argued:

> There is a limited number of common human problems for which all peoples must at all times find some solution. ... All alternatives of all solutions are present in all societies at all times but are differentially preferred. (1961: 10)

The preferred solutions represent a culture's values.

So all types of norms and behaviours exist in all cultures, but there is a tendency for certain norms to be more common in one culture than another. This is how we can usefully talk about cultural differences between countries, while at the same time not being able to say that any particular individual will exhibit specific preferences. It's helpful to know the valid tendencies, but we must always deal with each person as a unique individual. Also, cultures and subcultures evolve over time and are not monoliths.

Rather than trying to identify 'accurate' ratings of our own or other cultures, we need to raise our awareness of the various types of difference that exist, so that we can think and have dialogue in a more nuanced way. The dimensions models of Hofstede and Rosinski are an excellent tool for achieving that.

To be culturally and politically effective, we need to be aware of our preferences and norms, understand the norms of those around us, and design and implement effective high-integrity strategies and actions to reach our goals.

So, how do different cultural dimensions impact organisational politics?

Rosinski's Cultural Orientations Framework

In this chapter, we will follow the structure of Philippe Rosinski's Cultural Orientations Framework as it is the most comprehensive classification of cultural dimensions (see Table 3.1). We would like to thank Philippe for sharing his views in an interview with us in preparation for the writing of this book. Although in this section we use some examples from national cultural differences, remember that these dimensions can be used to identify and understand any types of difference in organisational culture.

Table 3.1 The Cultural Orientations Framework

Categories	Dimensions	Description
Sense of Power and Responsibility	Control/ Harmony/ Humility	*Control*: People have a determinant power and responsibility to forge the life they want
		Harmony: Strive for balance and harmony with nature
		Humility: Accept inevitable natural limitations
Time Management Approaches	Scarce/ Plentiful	*Scarce*: Time is a scarce resource. Manage it carefully!
		Plentiful: Time is abundant. Relax!
	Monochronic/ Polychronic	*Monochronic*: Concentrate on one activity and/or relationship at a time
		Polychronic: Concentrate simultaneously on multiple tasks and/or relationships
	Past/Present/ Future	*Past*: Learn from the past. The present is essentially a continuation or a repetition of past occurrences
		Present: Focus on the 'here and now' and short-term benefits
		Future: Have a bias towards long-term benefits. Promote a far-reaching vision
Definitions of Identity and Purpose	Being/Doing	*Being*: Stress living itself and the development of talents and relationships
		Doing: Focus on accomplishments and visible achievements
	Individualistic/ Collectivistic	*Individualistic*: Emphasise individual attributes and projects
		Collectivistic: Emphasise affiliation with a group

Table 3.1 (*continued*)

Categories	Dimensions	Description
Organisational Arrangements	Hierarchy/ Equality	*Hierarchy*: Society and organisations must be socially stratified to function properly
		Equality: People are equals who often happen to play different roles
	Universalist/ Particularist	*Universalist*: All cases should be treated in the same universal manner. Adopt common processes for consistency and economies of scale
		Particularist: Emphasise particular circumstances. Favour decentralisation and tailored solutions
	Stability/ Change	*Stability*: Value a static and orderly environment. Encourage efficiency through systematic and disciplined work. Minimise change and ambiguity, perceived as disruptive
		Change: Value a dynamic and flexible environment. Promote effectiveness through adaptability and innovation. Avoid routine, perceived as boring
	Competitive/ Collaborative	*Competitive*: Promote success and progress through competitive stimulation
		Collaborative: Promote success and progress through mutual support, sharing of best practices and solidarity
Notions of Territory and Boundaries	Protective/ Sharing	*Protective*: Protect yourself by keeping personal life and feelings private (mental boundaries), and by minimising intrusions in your physical space (physical boundaries)
		Sharing: Build closer relationships by sharing your psychological and physical domains
Communication Patterns	High Context/ Low Context	*High Context*: Rely on implicit communication. Appreciate the meaning of gestures, posture, voice and context
		Low Context: Rely on explicit communication. Favour clear and detailed instructions

(continued)

Table 3.1 (*continued*)

Categories	Dimensions	Description
	Direct/Indirect	*Direct*: In a conflict or with a tough message to deliver, get your point across clearly at the risk of offending or hurting
		Indirect: In a conflict or with a tough message to deliver; favour maintaining a cordial relationship at the risk of misunderstanding
	Affective/ Neutral	*Affective*: Display emotions and warmth when communicating. Establishing and maintaining personal and social connections are key
		Neutral: Stress conciseness, precision and detachment when communicating
	Formal/ Informal	*Formal*: Observe strict protocols and rituals
		Informal: Favour familiarity and spontaneity
Modes of Thinking	Deductive/ Inductive	*Deductive*: Emphasise concepts, theories and general principles. Then, through logical reasoning, drive practical applications and solutions
		Inductive: Start with experiences, concrete situations and cases. Then, using intuition, formulate general models and theories
	Analytical/ Systemic	*Analytical*: Separate a whole into its constituent elements. Dissect a problem into smaller chunks
		Systemic: Assemble the parts into a cohesive whole. Explore connections between elements and focus on the whole system

Organisational Arrangements

Under the category of 'Organisational Arrangements', Rosinski offers four dimensions: equality vs. hierarchy, universalist vs. particularist, stability vs. change and competitive vs. collaborative. Where an organisation's values sit on these dimensions will have a significant impact on how politics is experienced.

In cultures that value *hierarchy*, you may well lack the power to get things done on your own. The need to identify who has power is critical, and individuals need to build alliances in order to achieve their goals. In cultures that emphasise equality, individuals can be more direct in presenting their ideas and expect to get a fair hearing regardless of their position. In hierarchical cultures, people find it easier to share ideas with people at the same level in the organisation, rather than bouncing them off more senior people.

Hierarchy (or what Hofstede terms 'power distance') is one of the clearest ways in which culture impacts organisational politics. In a high power distance culture, it is expected that power is distributed unequally. This affects both formal and informal power. Employees often expect to respect and admire leaders both inside and outside work. I have coached British expatriates who have been working in multinational companies in a high power distance, hierarchical local culture. The British expatriates wanted to socialise, relax and get drunk with their team members on a Friday evening and would expect normal business relations to be back in place on Monday morning. However, they discovered that this didn't work, as they had lost the respect of their colleagues by partying and drinking with them. It was very hard for them to regain this lost respect and that greatly limited their ability to deliver on their organisational goals. Their political power was damaged.

In *universalist* cultures, people believe that all cases should be treated in the same way, based on common principles. In contrast, in *particularist* cultures, people believe that individual circumstances dictate how ideas and practices should be applied, so designing solutions for individual cases is much more acceptable. If you are trying to win support for a proposal in a universalist culture, then it is important to align it to commonly held principles and processes.

Cultures that value change are much more likely to be open to new and innovative ideas, whereas organisations based on *stability* will expect more systematic and disciplined approaches that minimise disruption.

In *competitive* cultures, it is much more acceptable to look for progress through competitive stimulation and to have competition between individuals and teams. If the culture is more *collaborative*, then you will need to emphasise sharing and solidarity and demonstrate mutual support.

Identity and Purpose

Under the category of 'Identity and Purpose', Rosinski lists two dimensions: individualistic vs. collectivistic and being vs. doing. In a more collectivist culture, it is essential to pay more attention to relationships and to align effectively with groups and subgroups. In a more individualistic culture, it is considered normal for people to act on their own and to have more individual accountability for tasks and projects. Likewise in *doing* cultures, it is more usual for people to focus on their accomplishments and visible achievements, whereas being cultures place more emphasis on relationships.

For all of the above dimensions, we need to think what are the norms for the culture of the organisation that we and our clients are operating in. Once we have understood that, we can decide on the most appropriate behaviours that will lead to success.

At one point earlier in my career, I managed teams of consultants in both China and the USA. In a team meeting in Beijing I praised one of the team for the great work she had done with one of our clients. She came to me afterwards and asked me never to do that again as it embarrassed her to be singled out from the group. China is much more collaborative and collectivist, whereas team members in the US tend to be more individualistic and competitive. I noticed some colleagues in the US were less open to share information and successes with other team members than their counterparts in China. Turning activities into a competition increased engagement. When we are planning high integrity activities within these cultures, these are important dimensions to consider.

Communication Patterns

There are four dimensions within 'Communication Patterns': high context vs. low context (based on the work of Edward Hall, 1976), direct vs. indirect, affective vs. neutral and formal vs. informal.

In low context cultures, the words just mean what they say, no more, no less. In high context cultures, how they are said, what is not said, when they are said, the tone of voice, who is on the email cc (or the bcc!), all have significant impact on meaning. High context cultures can be perceived as more political, and someone moving from a low context to a high context culture is likely to overlook many of the nuances that exist in communication because they are not used to noticing them. I've coached German nationals working in Turkey who have experienced this shift from typically low context to high context communication. By helping to focus their awareness on the context around messages they are giving and receiving, they have become more successful working in their new environment.

Alternatively, people who are used to a high context style of communication can have difficulty when switching to a low context culture. They may be looking for nuance or meaning that the speaker hasn't intended. I remember a case of a British CFO working with a large multinational that had just acquired a major Turkish business. In a town hall meeting in Istanbul, he was asked if there would be any redundancies. He replied: 'we have no plans for any redundancies'. In a meeting soon after with the senior finance team, I was asked, 'you're British, what did he really mean?'. People used to working in a high context culture such as Turkey will look for hidden meanings and try to interpret messages to understand what someone 'really' means. The potential for misunderstanding between high and low context cultures is significant and when thinking about politics, or 'the informal use of power', we need to pay attention to these differences. If you are used to low context communication but are working with high context people, you need to be aware that your words and actions will be analysed for hidden meaning and you may well need to communicate more than you are used to in order to be effective.

The *formality* of communication and other work practices is changing quickly and this was accelerated by the Covid-19 pandemic. There are now huge differences between countries and organisations around the world. Is it appropriate to join a video call in a T-shirt? How formally should you communicate by email or by phone? The impact of your messages will be weakened or even undermined if your level of formality seems inappropriate to the people you are engaging with.

Similarly, some cultures expect to communicate with emotions (*affective*), while others expect communication to remain *neutral* – detached and factual. And in some organisations very *direct* communication is encouraged, whereas in others it can make people uncomfortable.

To achieve our organisational goals, we have to communicate effectively, and we need to adapt to the communication preferences of the organisational culture(s) we are working with to be successful. All four of the above dimensions are important. In addition to these dimensions, some organisations tend to prioritise written communication and others oral. What will be most effective as an email in some cultures will be a WhatsApp message in others, and a phone or video call in still others. Communication styles need to be considered for effective behaviour in meetings and presentations as well. When joining a new organisation or division, it is important to learn what the preferred communication patterns are in that culture.

Sense of Power and Responsibility

Under Rosinski's category of 'Sense of Power and Responsibility', there are three values: control, harmony and humility. Cultures that value humility believe in accepting natural limitations, and those that focus on harmony believe that we should look for balance and harmony with nature and in our relationships. Those that emphasise control believe that people have more power and responsibility to determine the life they want to lead. It is all too easy to see North American cultures as tending towards control and many Asian cultures emphasising harmony or humility, but we need to beware of stereotyping individuals or groups. Thinking about whether your organisational culture values harmony or humility, or whether the company's cultural heroes are individuals who have forged their own destiny, will guide you on politically effective courses of action.

When something has gone wrong at work, these differences about power and responsibility are often exposed. Did the mistake 'just happen', should individuals be humble about their limitations or should we aim to have more control of events? People from different cultures have different, deeply held assumptions about these issues and lack of awareness of others' views can lead to misunderstanding and conflict.

Notions of Territory and Boundaries

There is just one dimension under 'Notions of Territory and Boundaries', that of protective vs. sharing. As a British person working for many years in a Mediterranean culture, I have experienced the clash of my values of the importance of private personal and mental space versus the view that closer relationships should be built by sharing psychological and physical space.

Modes of Thinking

The domain of 'Modes of Thinking' includes two dimensions: deductive vs. inductive and analytical vs. systemic. In terms of politics, these become particularly relevant when making arguments in support of a particular view. Deductive cultures emphasise concepts, theories and general principles, whereas inductive cultures argue from lived experience of individual cases, based on which general models may be built. Again, we need to adapt our styles of influencing and persuasion to the preferred way of thinking in the culture in which we are operating.

Analytical cultures tend to dissect an issue into smaller pieces, whereas systemic cultures explore connections between elements and focus on the whole system.

Time Management Approaches

In Chapter 2 on political astuteness, we talked about the importance of timing. Under the domain of 'Time Management Approaches', Rosinski lists three dimensions: scarce vs. plentiful, monochronic vs. polychronic and past/present/future. In some cultures, time is seen as *scarce* (time is money, manage it carefully), whereas in others it is seen as *plentiful* (relax!). Some cultures are *monochronic* (do one thing at a time and in order), while others are *polychronic* (do multiple things at once). Rosinski also notes that cultures tend to focus more on one of the *past, present* or *future*. To achieve your goals within and across organisations, you need to engage with their sense of time. In particular, some organisations prioritise talking about future plans, others on executing in the present, while some like to talk more about their heritage and learning from past success. You won't achieve your goals if you spend a lot of time talking about the past with a team or organisation that prioritises the future. If you are working in an organisation where setting 15-minute online meetings is seen as normal, you need to engage with that way of working to achieve your goals.

Hofstede's Cultural Dimensions

Hofstede's dimensions of individualism vs. collectivism and power distance have been covered under Rosinski's 'Organisational Arrangements' and 'Identity and Purpose' domains above. Another two of Hofstede dimensions deserve closer attention. Hofstede talks about masculine vs. feminine cultures. I believe this is simpler to understand as 'achievement vs. relationship'. (This is similar to Rosinski's being vs. doing dimension.)

While I was working with a Turkish multinational that acquired a large German company, the dimension of achievement vs. relationship presented a real challenge. Although as always there were many individual differences, typically the German employees were more focused on getting their work done, on time, whereas their new Turkish colleagues would pay more attention to maintaining relationships. A German team member was frustrated with a Turkish team member who was late to finish a task because they were dealing with a friend's personal issue on the phone. The Turkish colleague asked how they should have dealt with the situation, should they have ignored their friend in need? The German team member said because of the tight deadline, they simply wouldn't have answered the phone! In this case, the culture of the acquisition was managed well, but there was a risk that at worst the Germans would see the Turks as disorganised and missing deadlines and that the Turks would see the Germans as unfeeling and robotic.

To apply our political astuteness in a complex environment of conflict and contest, we need to pay a lot of attention to this dimension and give due importance to relationships if we are operating in a more relationship-focused culture. For example, I worked with some British executives who acquired a large Turkish organisation and after several months it became clear that the senior local leadership was not fully engaged. I ran some focus groups with the most senior Turkish leaders and they explained that they knew nothing about their new leaders as people. They described them as 'black boxes', with no personal items or photos on their desks, and not attending the company happy hours after work. When I spoke to some of the British leaders, they explained that they only expected to be in Turkey for six months to work on the integration project and wanted to spend time outside of work with their families who were adapting to their new environment. The British *achievement* focus in a Turkish *relationship*-oriented culture meant that the British leaders were not able to exercise informal political power effectively because they didn't engage people. Unfortunately, in this case the problem continued for some time, and the organisation only really flourished when a Turkish CEO was appointed some time later.

Hofstede's dimension of high vs. low uncertainty avoidance is one of the hardest to explain or understand. This dimension is not about the level of uncertainty or ambiguity in a culture but about how that uncertainty affects people. In *high uncertainty* avoidance cultures, lack of certainty causes anxiety, which leads people to set rules or make quick decisions to resolve the uncertainty. The two cultures I'm most familiar with are at opposite ends of this scale. Turkey scores highly on Hofstede's uncertainty avoidance dimension while the UK does not. In high uncertainty avoidance cultures, people are likely to be less comfortable saying 'I don't know' or working in ambiguous structures with multiple reporting lines. I have coached British managers working in Turkey who have needed to pay particular attention to this. When their teams ask for clear guidance and more structure about how they work, the leaders can struggle. I once worked with a British leader who told his Turkish team to 'ask for forgiveness not permission'. This is a worthy aim, but when it goes against strong cultural norms, it is challenging for at least some of the team.

Again, to be politically effective and reach our goals we need to pay due attention to the culture we are working in or with. This does not mean we have to adopt local norms. It does mean, however, that we need to be aware of the challenges we are presenting to others and we have to be prepared to put in the work to communicate more about our expectations and make it safe for people to act in the way we would like them to.

In high uncertainty avoidance cultures, leaders typically need to give more clarity around their goals and aims and how they want to achieve them, if they are to bring colleagues with them.

It is clear from some of the examples above that we often need to think about more than one dimension at once in terms of how we will be politically successful. The different dimensions interact and can intensify each other. For example, in a hierarchical and group-oriented (collectivist) culture, it is even more challenging for individuals to speak out or challenge their bosses. If that culture is also relationship-oriented, uncertainty-avoiding and communicates with high context, then political astuteness is even more vital for an employee to successfully challenge senior leaders.

In cultures that are hierarchical, group-oriented, relationship-focused and uncertainty-avoiding, it is important to 'socialise an idea' – that is, to present it informally to a number of people to get them to engage with it before formally recommending a proposal. In more achievement-oriented, lower power distance cultures, this can be seen as a waste of time and even be viewed with suspicion.

One of the culture-related complaints that I hear most often in hierarchical, uncertainty-avoiding organisations is that a manager's boss has spoken to the manager's team members without them being present. In some cultures, 'skip level meetings' are completely normalised, whereas in others they are considered a threat to a manager's autonomy. Again, to achieve our organisational goals we have to keep these issues in mind, and again the usual solution is sensitivity and lots of communication about process – which again some cultures will find unnecessary!

The most politically competent leaders are often also highly culturally competent. As coaches and mentors, we can raise people's awareness of where they and others sit on these different cultural dimensions and work with them to plan appropriate political actions. As well as using Hofstede's and Rosinski's dimensions to identify elements of a culture which impact politics, we can also look at some more specific indicators such as particular cultural norms within an organisation. Some companies have a history of embracing failure and experimentation, others place absolute priority on consumer experience, while still others prioritise employee wellbeing.

Companies with a strong engineering heritage and culture have often adopted Six Sigma and other Japanese-influenced process improvement models which aim to identify specific process weaknesses and make systematic improvements. Other cultures may prefer to focus on stories of archetypes or typical consumers, and build change programmes around particular success stories. Whether to focus more on what is working or on areas to improve is another way in which cultures differ.

Once we have considered where an organisation sits on the dimensions of culture, and what an individual's preferences in terms of cultural norms are, we can turn to look at what will be the most effective political behaviours in this context and what is and is not possible within the organisational system.

Understanding the cultural context of politics in an organisation

Throughout all of this discussion, one question predominates: 'What factors influence what can be done and who it can be done by?' Teasing out the factors that relate to simple practicalities (such as inadequate resources) from those that are more subtle helps reveal the presence of cultural politics. And once we know it's there, we can begin to understand and work with it.

Given that culture permeates everything in an organisational system, it's important to reveal, as far as possible, the interplay between them. We can approach this in one of two ways. The first is to use examples of, say, situational conflict or change resistance to extract themes relating to politics and/or culture. In other words, to approach the issue from the specific. The second is to map the culture and the political landscape and then explore the points of intersection and divergence.

Questions a coach can ask to elucidate the culture include:

- What are the narratives that underpin expectations of politics in this organisation?
- How do the stated values align (or not) with the values in action/actual behaviours?
- What responsibility do the leaders take for the political climate?
- How approachable are leaders? How comfortable do people feel with them?
- How does the organisation deal with mistakes and failure?
- Where in the organisation do the role models for positive and negative political behaviours reside?
- Who are the heroes of this organisation's stories?
- What stories are told of notable successes or failures?
- How are rules bent or broken here?
- Does reputational risk get discussed, and when?
- Who benefits most and least from the current political system?
- What behaviours are seen as the most taboo in this culture?
- What do people have to do to succeed here?
- What gets people fired?
- What is not discussed here?

- How do people deal with not knowing or not being sure about something?
- What does the current political system contribute to the sum of human happiness?
- What is the role of shame in how things are now?

Integrating cultural and political awareness

So what have we learnt in this chapter? Both Hofstede's and Rosinski's dimensions give us a nuanced, research-based way of comparing cultures. Hofstede's work provides data on many different countries around the world.

Some will argue that certain cultures (i.e. those with high power distance and more of a group and relationship focus) are 'more political' than others. Although I understand the logic in this, I don't find it helpful. All cultures work with informal power, hidden agendas and alliance building. So, I prefer to say that the way politics works and is expressed is simply different in different cultures. We tend to be accustomed or blind to the hidden ways of working in our own culture and therefore more likely to see foreign cultures as more political than our own.

We can talk of intercultural competence, and this is closely aligned with political competence. To achieve this, it is helpful to know the specifics of a culture we are working in or with. What is probably more useful and certainly of more long-term use is to be aware of the different types of cultural difference that exist. When we have a deeper understanding of the ways cultures vary in terms of organisational arrangements, attitudes to power and styles of communication, we will be primed to recognise those factors more quickly and effectively in our working lives. The other key factor and perhaps the most useful of all, is to be aware of our own cultural preferences, and to recognise that our preferences are no more valid or natural than those of anyone else.

Once we are aware of our own preferences and the norms in the organisation(s) we are working with, we can then design and implement effective high-integrity political strategies to achieve our goals.

Intercultural competence is similar to political astuteness. It is also similar to coaching competence. Many coaches demonstrate the skills of awareness, good listening, asking questions, checking for understanding, empathy, curiosity and paying respectful attention to differences. These are the same skills that people need to develop to manage organisational politics effectively in different cultural contexts, so coaches are ideally placed to help their clients further develop these skills.

As coaches and mentors, if we engage with organisational politics with this awareness and sensitivity, and encourage the same in our clients, we are much more likely to help them and their organisations achieve their goals effectively and with integrity.

References

Hall, E. (1976) *Beyond Culture*. New York: Doubleday.

Hofstede, G. (2001) *Culture's Consequences: Comparing Values, Behaviours, Institutions and Organizations Across Nations*, 2nd edition. London: Sage.

Hofstede, G. and Hofstede, G.J. (2010) *Cultures and Organizations: Software for the mind*, revised edition. New York: McGraw-Hill.

Kluckhohn, F. and Strodtbeck, F. (1961) *Variations in Value Orientations*. Evanston, IL: Row, Peterson.

Rosinski, P. (2003) *Coaching Across Cultures: New tools for leveraging national, corporate and professional differences*. London: Nicholas Brealey.

Rosinski, P. (2010) *Global Coaching: An integrated approach for long-lasting results*. London: Nicholas Brealey.

4 Power misused in organisational politics

Lise Lewis

The word 'subculture' tends to conjure a vision of murky depths where beliefs or interests are at variance with those of the wider culture. This potential underbelly of an organisation is where some like to savour the meandering of intricate labyrinths, seeking out kindred spirits, intent on plotting subterfuge that disrupts those not similarly minded – think of Iago's character destruction of Desdemona playing on Othello's susceptibility to jealousy, inciting him to murder his beloved wife:

> *Though I do hate him as I do hell pains, Yet, for necessity of present life, I must show out a flag and sign of love – Which is indeed but sign.*
> — Othello (I.i156)

Transferring this scenario to an organisational setting describes those intent on undermining the potency of leadership and co-workers. Those who target imagined weaknesses of co-workers use innuendo and rumour as strategic partners that camouflage a determination to rise to the top, ingratiate oneself or at least gain credibility for personal agendas.

The following extract illustrates a parallel in organisations when referencing archetypes: 'stories, beliefs, rituals and myths of … culture may fuel the archetype … The Warrior … and its Shadow, [which] seeks to hide and disown (Pearson, 1991) … Pearson refers to, "the villain who uses Warrior skills for personal gain without thought of morality, ethics, or the good of the whole group" (Pearson, 1991: 16)' (cited by Phillips, 2018: 87).

Other chapters in this book advocate the merits of organisational politics (see Chapters 2 and 3). This chapter seeks to uncover and shed light on the undermining 'darker' or 'shadow' side of organisational culture that, although evident and often tolerated, seems to cause no more than disgruntled asides alluding to unfair practices and disturbed values. The clever manipulation of others by those practised in the skill can go unrecognised, remaining invisible as a disruptor of organisational performance. This 'darker' side of politics resources those pursuing routes to self-aggrandisement through irregular means and who willingly ignore the ethical implications of subversive practices.

The darker side of politics reflects the shadow side of personality that psychologists refer to as the 'dark triad':

- *Narcissists*, who can be boastful, arrogant, lacking in empathy and hypersensitive to criticism.
- *Machiavellians*, who may be duplicitous, manipulative, self-interested and lack both emotion and morality.
- *Psychopaths*, who also lack empathy or remorse, exhibit antisocial behaviour, and can be manipulative and volatile – this is not to suggest they are psychopaths.

Let's take a reality check on the 'darker' side of organisational politics.

Whether this practice is recognised, tolerated or unconsciously ignored, the consequences cause damage to the wellbeing of those impacted and to organisations when people divert energy to create coping strategies. Enlightened employers are aware of and fulfil a legal responsibility to do everything reasonably practicable to make sure that employees' health and safety are protected. A supplementary benefit is strengthening the psychological contract through being a caring employer.

The espoused culture

'Experiential reality suggests that political behavior is a pervasive force in organizational life' (Witt, 1992: 1). Office politics can't be avoided, is necessary and can positively influence organisational performance. Research by Treadway et al. 'demonstrated that individuals with positive performance were more likely to possess higher levels of interpersonal power if they were high in political skill' (2011: 1529). A positive result for endorsing 'political savvy' and reinforcing that relational leadership gains greater traction in employee engagement than outdated leadership styles.

David Clutterbuck's model on culture comprises three overlapping circles (Figure 4.1):

Figure 4.1 David Clutterbuck's model on culture.

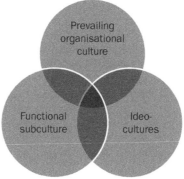

1 Prevailing organisational culture.
2 Functional subcultures (e.g. purchasing often operates with its own set of values that may not align with the corporate values).
3 Ideo-cultures being the influence of powerful individuals.

Organisational politics used for ulterior motives adversely affect employees, potentially to the point of burnout, when feeling the strain of wasted energy in appeasing those with the ability to create barriers. A vivid memory stays with me of employees outwardly extolling the virtues of the workplace only to admit, in one-to-one coaching conversations, a fear of not 'toeing the company line' impacting on career development, or worse still, continuity of employment. A personal memory is when a female line manager's appetite for calling end-of-day meetings necessitated hasty childcare arrangements. This was before family-friendly policies existed and when home commitments were not expected to 'interfere' with availability for impromptu discussions. David Clutterbuck makes a distinction between 'malevolent' politics intended to benefit only a few or even one person, 'benevolent' politics that encourages results by consensus and 'negligent' politics where issues are avoided. Applying this distinction to the scenario shared here, it is both 'malevolent' in satisfying the line manager and 'negligent' by 'overlooking' I had childcare responsibilities. A 'benevolent' result for me would be to have discussed the feasibility of meeting 'after hours'; whether the topic can wait until the next day or is so important that alternative childcare arrangements are necessary.

Gallo (2022) offers an alternative view in urging us to remember that our 'perspective is just one among many' and that as 'we all come to the workplace with different viewpoints and values', it's not necessarily realistic to expect – in this scenario – my manager to view this request for a late impromptu meeting in the same way that I did. We're asked to challenge ourselves with questions that include: 'How do I know that what I believe is true?' and 'What assumptions have I made?' In this scenario, I decided a safe option was to comply with the request based on pre-existing knowledge of how this leader anticipated agreement to her requests. I believed disagreement equalled a penalty and assumed lack of understanding for childcare responsibilities. Comparing my choice with Gallo's work is a reminder that this was my view only and not everyone sees things in the same way.

Legislation designed to challenge poor employment practices sadly cannot guarantee changes to mindset. A leadership culture defined by an unwritten 'like for like' recruitment policy perpetuates existing norms and maintains the status quo when unquestioned and unchallenged. Attempts to appease suggestions of modernisation practices may be given a 'lip service' of agreement displaying a willingness to acquiesce by adopting new practices that gradually fade into obscurity. 'What we see is not always what we get' and can erode trust in leadership.

What is the leader's intention – one of genuinely serving others or one of feeding their shadow side, or perhaps a combination of the two? Being human possibly exhibits all aspects of the public face. As coaches, might we be drawn into a parallel process with our clients and be cautious about 'who we are'? Are we consciously or unconsciously drawn to impress and collude with leader motivations, by mirroring ego drivers that reinforce the shadow side of protecting our working agreement? Or, do we role-model ethical practice and invite the leader into a conversation of self-discovery encouraging change towards authenticity?

Our survey completed by leaders saw office politics 'to be avoided at all costs' or a 'necessary evil'. When leaders role-model what becomes an organisational cultural norm in approving the 'darker' side of politics, might this encourage a ripple effect endorsing potentially damaging behaviours as acceptable practice? Ninety per cent of our survey leader respondents rated 'political astuteness' (being politically aware and able to work with different power relationships and conflicting objectives) as 'very important' or 'quite important' in the workplace. People adept at balancing such complexity survive and thrive in organisations, are politically aware and have excellent performance. Although the phrase 'necessary evil' may sound negative, I recall a recent coaching conversation when the reality of a situation, although unpalatable to some, was recognised as being more expedient. Existing working practices accepted as the norm and informed by culture, necessitated finding a solution that would ease a way forward for a higher purpose. In this scenario, the end result was felt to be more important than challenging an impregnable position that would create barriers. Although decisions made in the interests of expediency do not preclude revisiting the barriers to encourage shared understanding that drives change.

The invisible subculture

Consistency of comment from the survey can, if interpreted as such, reinforce the potential for the 'darker' side of office politics:

- *It's always present*: it can be clean, polluted or extremely polluted, signalling the health of the organisation.
- *It's a display of power dynamics*: typifying covert and overt use of power to achieve objectives.
- *It's a way to influence outcomes*: knowing what relationships are important and how to nurture engagement.
- *It's a way to advance self-interests*: reinforcing the cliché, 'it's not what you know, it's who you know'.

The complex nature of being human means that being authentic is not always preferred, or deemed possible by those feeling disadvantaged, or even a sensible option for those fearing consequences. Life has changed for humans – how we attempted to survive in the past no longer sufficiently protects us now (read more about this in Chapter 5). Protecting ourselves, wherever our location, from those perceived as 'different' and possibly a threat, kept us safe. The workplace is inevitably becoming multicultural when operating in a global market. Banaji and Greenwald (2016) talk of 'mindbugs' that slant how we see, remember, reason and judge to reveal a disparity between our intentions and ideals versus our behaviour and actions. We experience a disconnect between our inner minds and outward actions. Our good intentions of lived values of fairness and inclusivity, and behaving as social beings, are sabotaged by our sensed reality of surviving in the modern workplace. Survival signals from the past are resurrected to warp our behaviour and keep us safe. We may admire whistle-blowers, although avoid the risk of attracting a similar fate of perhaps isolation and blame that lack of support attracts. Why risk being ostracised and perhaps lose employment for the sake of 'being right'? What might be another route to change that opens a dialogue offering mutual understanding and compromise?

Advocating political debate encourages transparency and normalises the activity as signalling a healthy organisation welcoming mutuality of diverse thinking. Among the tactics that Kteily and Finkel (2022) recommend for implementation are:

- Educating people about naïve realism and how to put their own biases into perspective.
- Establishing forums where people with different political views can listen to each other with curiosity and work together to find common ground. A tactic we have found useful starts with agreeing the positive outcome that we all want to happen, such as fair processes for promotions. It then looks at the range of approaches and solutions that could be applied – both from the opposing perspective and from other perspectives. Finally, it seeks to identify combinations of approach that would lead to a more satisfactory outcome for everyone.
- Encouraging people to take the perspective of a neutral third party.
- Engaging both sides in creating metrics that they commonly see as fair.

How the 'darker' side of politics manifests

Let's acknowledge again that being politically savvy has its advantages. We can 'reality check' our ideas, prime others about relevant data for strategic meetings, elicit advice, leverage networks, and more. The greatest advantage accrues when we are adept at growing alliances and being willing to accept that political engagement is necessary and sometimes essential for 'oiling the wheels' for both personal and business agendas to be accepted. Agendas are just implemented or accepted more easily when perceived and real boundaries can be eliminated before decision meetings are held; this doesn't necessarily equal unethical practices.

Those without the ability, inclination or desire to engage with organisational politics for whatever reason are likely at some time to be excluded. Again, this may or may not be an issue. When exclusion does become an issue is when the 'darker' side of organisational politics finds fertile ground. Presumably, this happens whatever the role one has in the organisation, although we may assume that those at the top of the organisation have realised the potency of political savvy. Comparing Mahatma Gandhi with Donald Trump, both may be considered 'politically savvy', although by different routes and with opposing values.

Leaders encouraging a positive political environment suggests seeking a high level of consciousness. Figure 4.2 typifies leadership profiles that engage and motivate, and what's to disagree, except how well this mirrors reality? Might it be idealistic and naïve to believe that people will always put the needs of the business and others before self?; perhaps a dilution of such altruism is more feasible especially when recognising egoistic gratification. Will the leader who seeks compliance by manipulating charisma (Conger and Kanungo, 1998) mask the anticipated personal benefit and create unsafe boundaries, causing anxiety and ambivalence for those recognising the screen of deception? This incompatibility of values between the leader and those beneficial to the business demonstrates disparity between lived and espoused values.

The ideal scenario is where the leader's personal values are attuned (highly aligned) with the values of the organisation (Figure 4.3). The leader who pursues personal goals above encouraging collaboration, will likely limit nurturing alliances with those perceived as challenging, defensive and controlling, preferring perhaps to encourage competitiveness between workers as a way of generating increased productivity. I recall a similar scenario in a previous career as a branch manager for a national recruitment consultancy. My natural untrained leadership style was one of encouraging harmony and collaboration towards a common purpose of generating income, leveraging strengths and creating a fun place to work. Our branch had a healthy level of converting permanent and temporary placements. Managers were

Figure 4.2 One 'way of being' a leader.

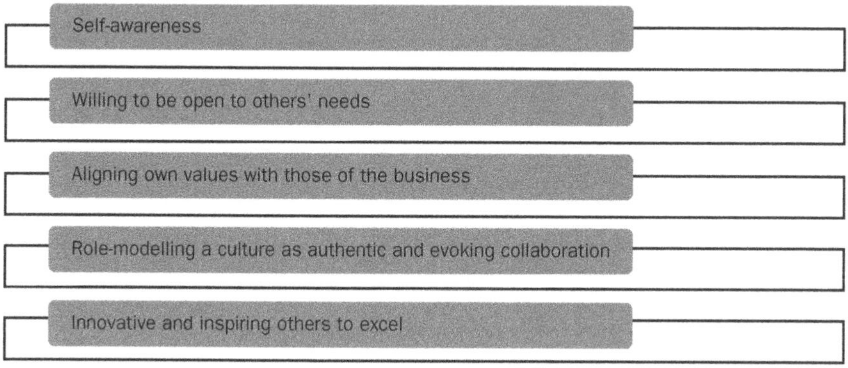

Figure 4.3 Alignment with values framework.

occasionally invited to a local café with a regional group director to review branch performance and encourage higher sales. The message was clear: encourage competition between the recruitment consultants to increase placements equalling progressively higher turnover for the branch. Delivery was direct and forceful and left no doubt that this was an instruction to step up. I asked colleagues for their thoughts; they were unimpressed by the lack of organisational recognition for their efforts and one by one we left. None of us wished to feel harassed into manipulating companies to interview potential employees lacking the necessary skills or persuading applicants to attend interviews for positions mismatched with employment aspirations. Young and politically unaware, I followed my values. Would being politically aware have changed the outcome? Increasing income equalled higher bonuses for all branch employees, reflected well on managers and influenced progression within the company. Reflecting on this now, could I have chosen a different route? My answer is 'no'; did this make me politically unaware or ethically astute or both back then?

Power as an enabler of coercive behaviours

As a way of recognising the adverse impact of power, this section centres on negative elements of power misuse that affect people generally. Our survey suggested that office politics are 'best avoided' and the question is, what recourse is there for those affected by the misuse of power?

An enabler of having power or not having power stems from personal characteristics: race, gender, education, religion, accent, what we wear, presence and more with socialisation being a persuasive instigator of power attribution, based on bias and prejudice attributing to or diminishing the ability to gain or have power withheld. I recall the warning of the '60'-second interview bias prompting us to beware of 'first impressions'. It seems we now have no more than a 'blink of an eye' to make a first impression and we may not get a second chance. In this short space, others unconsciously decide about personality, what car we drive, where we go on holiday, the type of home we have and more; all to satisfy that part of our 'reptilian brain' hard-wired to keep us safe. Research by Willis and Todorov (2006) reveals that in a tenth of a second, we form an impression of a stranger from their face, and that lengthening the contact doesn't significantly alter first impressions. A sobering thought!

Scenarios of misplaced attribution of power rooted in prejudice

A colleague employed in the medical sector, whose presence was challenged by a senior consultant through an intermediary, described hearing: 'What is this person doing here? Get them out.' 'This person' was a person of colour employed as the most senior employee in the medical team allocated to this hospital case.

A meeting attended by two men and two women has a male notetaker. Two comments made by a woman were acknowledged by the group. Immediately following, a man rephrased what the woman had just said. This was recorded in the meeting notes alongside the male's name. A second contribution by another woman was attributed again to a man who offered the same explanation using the same language.

Misuse of personal power is within the capability of us all and we may like to pause here for a moment and reflect on when we've been tempted or actually engaged in manipulative behaviour to 'get what we want'. Is this morally unacceptable, or sensible practice for circumventing what appear to be unnecessary barriers? Think of the self-centred leader influenced by the sycophantic praise of those wishing to ingratiate their way up the ladder of promotion. Alternatively, does evading the attention of a narcissistic, ego-inflated, sometimes neurotic and psychopathic leader (Sinclair, 2007) make sense, for securing employment necessary for economic survival?

Power becomes addictive when the sensation released by dopamine offers the same chemical transmitter that brings pleasure. As with any addiction, the fix of another 'pleasure hit' motivates the need to access the stimulation repeatedly, often at any cost. Compulsion of this type leads to behaviours that appease the hungry mouth of addiction without compassion for the injuries sustained by others.

The work of French and Raven (1959) remains relevant. Their five types of leadership power, together with a sixth added later by Raven, offer context for the types of power influencing the downside of organisational politics (see Table 4.1). Although Types 1–3 are most likely to encourage the 'shadow' side of organisational politics, given certain conditions we see that Types 4–6 could invite a similar propensity for self-gratification.

Table 4.1 Six types of leadership power

Leadership type	Opportunity for damaging behaviour
1. Legitimate power based on position and expected compliance	Withdrawing or withholding approval
2. Reward power, from either bestowing tangible benefit or giving approval	Giving pay awards can reward, although reward generally only achieves compliance
3. Coercive power through threat	Either of physical or economic harm, or of disapproval or rejection
4. Referent power, derived from being well respected, whatever one's formal status	'Everyone admires JJ' and JJ uses this popularity to influence personal gain when alternative routes are inaccessible
5. Expert power, based on knowledge, skills and experience as evidenced by credentials	Creating a 'smoke screen' of inaccessible technical language to gain personal advantage
6. Informational power from having information that others need or want	Withholding knowledge to consolidate own position

From French and Raven (1959) with a later addition by Raven.

'Reflecting on how we use our power can stir up difficult emotions. Who wants to admit to how they try to influence and manipulate others to fit in with their sense of how the world should be?' (Campion, 2021: 10–13). While this statement may be true of many people, there is a sector of society with a desire to 'influence and manipulate others'. The work of Cislak et al. (2018) shows that we seek power when motivated to have control over others and especially to influence behaviour. Alternatively, personal need for control is satisfied through attaining 'high positions' increasing independence and autonomy.

Cislak et al. (2018) find that personal control 'tends to have positive interpersonal consequences' and argue whether power is necessarily corrupt. Three studies showed that 'perceptions of power' and 'personal control' may have opposite consequences:

- 'power over others' positively predicted aggressiveness and manipulation;
- 'personal control' predicted the opposite.

Developing what motivates the desire for 'power over others' sheds light on this basic human trait. The need for survival is well known as a driver for being part of a 'tribe' to protect against threat by offering safety in numbers. A hierarchy forms when the strongest and more capable of the tribe are recognised and achieve the status that naturally grants power. Once power is assigned, we have choices about how we use it. We can empower or disable.

Those intent on using power as a disabler may attract the attention of 'whistle-blowing' as an antidote to reduce the 'intensity' and possible damaging consequences of exercising power over others. The choice to speak out about adverse practices largely depends on whether there is trust that leadership will welcome information about potential problems. If there is a risk of termination of employment or of being labelled as a 'disruptor', it takes courage to voice unethical behaviours and malevolent practices continue to flourish. Whistle-blowing has mixed reviews; think of one being the accusations made against 'backstabbing' Rishi Sunak for resigning due to Boris Johnson's unacceptable behaviour. Research by Welch and Stubben (2020) offers an alternative, with findings showing that 'whistleblowers are crucial to keep firms healthy' and internal reports are 'credible' and 'valuable' as remedial indicators for damage limitation against adverse practices.

Where the real power lies in organisations

We can readily be seduced into believing power within an organisation exists in the status attributed to roles. This can be true, although one would be deluded if believing this is routine. Let's look beyond the organisational structure to reveal where the 'real' power lies in organisations.

What lies beneath the well-designed job profiles slotted into the organisational structure organigram?; what subcultures might we uncover?

We all know of a 'person of good intent' who connects us to the best person to resolve our question. What do we know about the person who slithers along the corridors of subterfuge weaving tales of innuendo to meet their own needs or undermine the reputation of others?

By the nature of their 'undercover activities', it can be very difficult to recognise those that wield power through being 'politically astute' with damaging intent. The first sign of undermining influences notably affecting leadership is commonly revealed by 'the element of surprise' that is difficult to challenge although realised as complicit behaviour. Think of the recent downfall of the UK's Prime Minister Boris Johnson precipitated by the resignations of two top ministers: Rishi Sunak, the Chancellor of the Exchequer, and Sajid Javid, the Health Secretary, who resigned within minutes of one another. More decisively, a flood of further resignations followed, with more than fifty Members of Parliament quitting cabinet roles or other government positions, including some appointed to replace those who had already resigned. Despite the Prime Minister's fight for survival, there was no escape from the magnitude of this challenge. Was the almost simultaneous combined resignation of two top ministers a coincidence or the climax of a carefully manoeuvred strategic ousting? 'It is also occasionally necessary for employees to work behind the scenes to build coalitions of believers in a new vision to convince others' (Jarrett, 2017). Subsequent activities both as large 'P' and small 'p' practices attempt to demonstrate where the 'real power' lies in the same political party.

Scenario from an executive

Then there are those who 'change the narrative' to suit their needs. A conversation was requested under the façade of curiosity to know more about a head of service's position on a topic for discussion in a future meeting. The day of the meeting arrived, the head of service presented their position expecting support, only to feel totally defeated by a distortion of their misused information, leaving their position compromised. The head of service, when sharing this duplicity, found it difficult – in fact, impossible – to challenge this person in a more senior role. Was this behaviour 'political savvy' or unethical, or both?

Whatever the motives of those enthusiastic about using alternative means for accelerating preferred outcomes, is there a case for being more alert to and conscious of one's own privilege either through personal attributes or position held?

Overt and covert reactions diluting coercion to engage

An article by Heifetz and Linsky (2002) reports how leaders can be too late to react to imminent threats when implementing difficult change initiatives. The challenge by others may be direct by engineering a shift that avoids discussion of the proposal. A more subtle approach might be diverting the leader's capacity with excessive, time-consuming detail. The agenda of those affected is to restore order and avoid the 'organisational disequilibrium' created by the initiative.

'Quiet' resistance as a diversionary political strategy is best explained as the person who says, 'Yes, of course – only too happy to make these changes – complete these tasks – take on this new assignment' – and so on. You get the idea and are probably well acquainted. The issue is that the person has no intention of delivering and despite reminders and offers of support, never seems to deliver on the promises made, usually avoided by a range of plausible excuses.

The challenges to change may be more about self-preservation, especially with the threat of job losses, status and personal benefits including pay. Low-level sabotage can be an effective form of protest by those disengaged with organisational plans. Change is difficult and projects fail to implement when insufficient planning is given to the emotional reaction that change provokes. Best-laid plans can be thwarted by those intent on finding ways of obstructing operations, especially when owners of 'point of delivery' knowledge. One of the most successful change management projects I experienced was one where a series of meetings were held with employees. These were consultation events in the widest sense. The reasons for change were detailed and observations invited. Suggestions were acted upon or detailed reasons given for those unable to implement with a further invitation to offer alternatives for resolution. The meetings were unhurried and gave space for adjusting to the impact and adoption of change – precontemplation, contemplation, preparation, action and maintenance (Prochaska and Velicer, 1997).

Power takes many forms and traditionally power and leadership are assumed to co-exist: to apply power, leaders must be able to influence decisions and control resources. Changes responding to the complexities of today's workplace introduce 'new power'. This is when several having power may shift the power base in a team, leading to team members having more power than the leader. A functioning team in this scenario depends fully on the team having a common purpose, members having a team not an individual mindset, transparency and enthusiasm for knowledge-sharing to avoid the disruption of fragmentation through personal political agendas.

Scenario from practice

At the start of a coaching programme, a client was strongly drawn to the technical aspects of the role and had no interest in the political scene. The client gradually acknowledged an unrealised skill in organisational politics. A willingness to challenge those wanting to take unjustified credit for high-profile projects sits comfortably with concessionary inclusion in minor projects to satisfy the need for recognition in a culture having this expectation. Talking through when it matters to challenge from a strong ethical base and when it's politically advantageous to accept giving credit helped find an acceptable resolution. Reflecting on this and similar scenarios recognises pitfalls and resolutions for championing diversity and inclusion when cultural norms for behaviours are not only acceptable but anticipated.

Summary of what coaches can do

The most important contribution of the role of coaching is to bring harmful issues from the shadows into the light and to support the redirection of culture towards collaboration and trust. If the narrative of coaching clients speaks of mistrusting others who appear self-serving and having hidden agendas masked by kindness, coaching helps to validate or invalidate this perception. Asking what happens to substantiate thoughts and feelings helps the client to gain a sense of reality that either authenticates or disproves perceptions. Working from this base regulates the coaching conversation towards being curious about barriers to act and possibilities for future intentions. 'Giving emphasis to mutually empowering work, to creating conditions that allow groups to flourish, and to promoting learning and innovation through connection as well as individually autonomous action' (Sinclair, 2007).

Efforts to sabotage organisational success sound self-defeating, so what encourages resistance to 'speaking out' about feelings of being disenfranchised? What will motivate those unaccustomed to nurturing support networks to engage with colleagues to find solutions that dilute the 'either/or' responses to confrontation and to find a win-win compromise?

Coaching conversations inevitably uncover issues stemming from entanglement in organisational politics and emerge when individual values and ethical or moral boundaries collide with a workplace event. How does the coach support their clients' psychological safety and encourage acceptance of personal power to influence and find a route that encourages disclosure?

Coaching helps to bring clarity that reveals the power structure existing within an organisation and how to work with this. Where might alliances be built and what might be within a client's scope of influence? Supporting clients to find a way of being honest about feelings when psychological safety exists, builds confidence to seek out and encourage collaborative networks.

We experience more complex working relationships now that the workplace has become increasingly culturally diverse. An internet search as a reflexive reaction for increasing cultural awareness, paints a broad picture generalising cultural norms. Inevitably this excludes recognising that the same nuances existing in our own culture also exist in others. We can equally be enticed into believing a shared language equals shared understanding. Vocabulary can be translated and interpreted to have different meanings beyond what is intended. Tone and volume of speech create harmony or encourage separation, creating distortions in communication and understanding. Intercultural competence is helped by coaching revealing blind spots and the pitfalls of making assumptions generated from the underlying influences of socialisation. Being politically astute is being honest and transparent about a natural cultural awareness deficit and shows a willingness to be receptive.

Political skills of a coach

- Political intelligence
- Integrity and ethical astuteness
- Unbiased sensitivity
- Systemic recognition.

Issues coaches can raise with leaders

- How might your own political leanings make you blind or intolerant towards other people's political views, insofar as they relate to issues in the workplace?
- What polarities of viewpoint may be causing conflict that undermines productivity?
- How can you be a role model for acknowledging and respecting other political views?

References

Banaji, M.R. and Greenwald, A.G. (2016) *Blind Spot: Hidden biases of good people*. New York: Bantam Books.

Campion, H. (2021) Know thy power!, *Coaching Perspectives*, 31: 10–13.

Cislak, A., Cichocka, A., Wojcik, A.D. and Frankowska, N. (2018) Power corrupts, but control does not: What stands behind the effects of holding high positions, *Personality and Social Psychology Bulletin*, 44 (6): 944–957.

Conger, J. and Kanungo, R. (1998) *Charismatic Leadership in Organizations*. San Francisco, CA: Jossey-Bass.

French, J.R.P., Jr. and Raven, B.H. (1959) The bases of social power, in D. Cartwright (ed.) *Studies in Social Power*. Ann Arbor, MI: The University of Michigan Press (pp. 150–167).

Gallo, A. (2022) How to navigate conflict with a coworker, *Harvard Business Review*, September/October. Available at: https://hbr.org/2022/09/how-to-navigate-conflict-with-a-coworker.

Heifetz, R. and Linsky, M. (2002) A survival guide for leaders, *Harvard Business Review*, June. Available at: https://hbr.org/2002/06/a-survival-guide-for-leaders.

Jarrett, M. (2017) The 4 types of organizational politics, *Harvard Business Review*, 24 April 24. Available at: https://hbr.org/2017/04/the-4-types-of-organizational-politics.

Kteily, N. and Finkel, E.J. (2022) Leadership in a politically charged age: What social psychology and relationship science can teach us about conflict in the workplace – and how to manage it, *Harvard Business Review*, July/August. Available at: https://hbr.org/2022/07/leadership-in-a-politically-charged-age.

Pearson, C.S. (1991) *Awakening the Heroes Within: Twelve archetypes to help us find ourselves and transform our world*. San Francisco, CA: Harper.

Phillips, K. (2018) Working with intense emotions, in E. Turner and S. Palmer (eds) *The Heart of Coaching Supervision: Working with reflection and self-care*. London: Routledge (pp. 83–104).

Prochaska, J.O. and Velicer, W.F. (1997) The Transtheoretical Model of Health Behavior Change, *American Journal of Health Promotion*, 12 (1): 38–48.

Sinclair, A. (2007) *Leadership for the Disillusioned: Moving beyond myths and heroes to leading that liberates*. Crows Nest, NSW: Allen & Unwin.

Treadway, D.C., Breland, J.W., Williams, L.M., Cho, J., Yang, J. and Ferris, G.R. (2011) Social influence and interpersonal power in organizations: Roles of performance and political skill in two studies, *Journal of Management*, 39 (6): 1529–1553.

Welch, K. and Stubben, S. (2020) Throw out your assumptions about whistleblowing, *Harvard Business Review*, 14 January. Available at: https://hbr.org/2020/01/throw-out-your-assumptions-about-whistleblowing.

Willis, J. and Todorov, A. (2006) First impressions: Making up your mind after a 100-ms exposure to a face, *Psychological Science*, 17 (7): 592–598.

Witt, L.A. (1992) *Organizational Politics, Participation in Decision Making, and Job Satisfaction*. Washington, DC: Office of Aviation Medicine, US Department of Transportation, Federal Aviation Administration. Available at: http://www.tc.faa.gov/its/worldpac/techrpt/AM92-17.pdf.

5 Fears and psychological safety

David Clutterbuck and Riddhika Khoosal

When people talk of an organisation having a 'political climate', they are usually referring to an environment that prevents them from being authentic. There is a vicious cycle here: such environments create low levels of psychological safety and low psychological safety creates negative political behaviours. The engine that prevents people being authentic and speaking up is *fear*. When we are afraid, we seek to protect ourselves. Expedience takes precedence over what we feel is 'right'. Raising issues that go against the prevailing politics becomes dangerous. Imposter syndrome (where people exert more and more control to avoid showing any weaknesses) thrives.

In contrast, creating a positive political climate requires the generation of high levels of psychological safety. This in turn allows people to be more authentic, to raise contentious issues, be true to their personal values and to feel less pressure to protect their reputation. In this chapter, we explore how leaders, with the help of coaches as needed, can build psychological safety for themselves and others – to achieve a positive political climate. We also present a fictional case study to illustrate some of the key themes.

What is psychological safety?

Amy Edmondson broadly defines psychological safety as:

> *a climate in which people are comfortable expressing and being themselves. More specifically, when people have psychological safety at work, they feel comfortable sharing concerns and mistakes without fear of embarrassment or retribution. They are confident that they can speak up and won't be humiliated, ignored, or blamed.* (2019: xvi)

William Kahn has described it as a sense of being 'able to show and employ one's self without fear of negative consequences to self-image, status, or career' (Kahn, 1990: 703–704). Both definitions stress the *absence* of climatic factors that stimulate anxiety, stress or fear. Symptoms of low psychological safety include lack of creative dialogue, hidden opinions, unwillingness to challenge the status quo, excessive compliance and stress. The flip side is the *presence* of interpersonal trust, empathetic curiosity and a deep sense of belonging. Symptoms of a positive psychological climate include high creativity, playfulness and collective self-honesty.

In both high and low psychological safety climates, there exist both internal and external narratives. For example:

External narrative

- Do people say what they think, or what they feel is the 'correct' thing to say?
- Do people challenge others' ideas directly or behind the scenes?
- Do people feel it is important to protect the identity they assume within this environment?

Internal narrative

- Do people spend time and energy calculating the consequences of speaking up?
- Do they rationalise conflicts of values rather than discuss them openly?
- Are they constantly on the look-out for dangers to avoid?

A survey by RVB Associates of 400 middle managers found that:

- 44% were unwilling to make suggestions and offer ideas for fear of being put down
- more than half thought that offering ideas to top management was a waste of time
- nearly one-third felt it was too threatening to offer contrarian ideas
- nearly half felt that, when they did offer ideas that were accepted, they did not get the credit.

Voice

The concept of psychological safety is also closely tied to voice (the degree to which people feel empowered to speak up and be listened to) and to trust.

Adam Grant of the University of Pennsylvania has researched effective strategies for achieving voice for several decades. In one study across manufacturing, service, retail and non-profit settings, he found that the more frequently employees voiced concerns and ideas upward, the less likely they were to receive raises and promotions over a two-year period. Faced with situations they feel are wrong, he finds that there are four strategies people can take. One is to do nothing and accept that you are powerless – maintaining the status quo. Another is to leave, which changes the situation for you but not for the organisation. Both these options are detrimental to the organisation. The potential for positive outcomes lies in either quiet persistence – going with the status quo but building an influence network that can eventually challenge it – or to speak up, with all the dangers that entails. Speaking up usually requires that people feel they can make a difference by doing so and that they care deeply about the issue. In a climate of low psychological safety, the belief that nothing will change tips the balance away from voice.

However, it is possible to increase voice at both the individual and collective levels. At a collective level, persistence can result in bringing together sufficient people with the same concerns to develop collective identity and influence. The 'me-too' movement is a classic example of this. At an individual level, people can learn how to achieve voice without damaging their careers. Grant argues that

> Intense emotions such as frustration, anger, and dissatisfaction often drive employees to speak up. Yet the very emotions that spur employees to express voice may compromise their ability to do so constructively, preventing managers from reacting favourably ... to speak up frequently and constructively, employees need knowledge about effective strategies for managing emotions. (2013: 1703)

Here lies a key role for coaches: helping clients develop the skills of speaking effectively with confidence.

Various studies suggest that, when people recognise and manage the fears they experience in a psychologically unsafe environment, they can develop strategies for overcoming those fears. Fear makes us pessimistic and excessively cautious, so we exaggerate the risks of speaking up (Kish-Gephart et al., 2009: 172; Milliken et al., 2003: 1469). The antidote is what is described as 'deep acting', which involves:

- Confronting one's fears and replacing them with a focus on the benefits of the desired change.
- Rehearsing the conversation that is needed, taking into account:
  - Content: what needs to be said
  - Context: when and how it should be said
  - Emotional regulation: practising the required emotions and the physiological supports for them (such as standing taller, with shoulders back).

Of course, sometimes a situation arises where there is a need to speak up spontaneously, without the opportunity to prepare. The academic literature refers to this as 'surface acting'. Equally reliant on emotional intelligence, these situations may backfire on us. The key is to use them as learning opportunities, gradually developing instinctive emotional regulation responses and a vocabulary that makes challenge less threatening to others and hence less likely to be received negatively.

In the discussion of our case study later in this chapter, we look more deeply at the fear instinct and how to manage it.

Trust

Trust helps to build psychological safety but it is not the same thing. Trust relates to expectations of another person's future intentions and behaviours. Psychological safety is about how people feel in the moment and is particularly associated with what happens in groups and teams. According to Edmondson (2019: 17), trust is about giving others the benefit of the doubt, while psychological safety relates to whether others will give you the benefit of the doubt when, for instance, you have asked for help or admit a mistake. The differences between the two concepts are summarised neatly by Tammy Turner in Table 5.1.

Table 5.1   Difference between psychological safety and trust (Turner, T. 2019) from the article The Importance of Psychological Safety in Team Coaching by Colm Murphy and Tammy Turner.

Psychological safety	Trust
Is a group construct	Is an individual construct
Measures if it's ok to openly share concepts and make mistakes	Measures if another can be counted on to do what they say they'll do
Measured by team members – they 'know' if the environment is safe	Measured by an individual about the other
Gives you as a contributing team member the benefit of the doubt	You give the other person the benefit of the doubt for getting things done

Reproduced with permission from Turner (2019).

In a situation of low psychological safety, knowing who you can and can't trust is an essential survival mechanism. The politics of trust attend to factors such as:

- When can I rely on others to speak up on my behalf or in support of my proposals?
- What pressures are they under that may cause them to act against my interests?
- What is their history of trustworthiness?
- What are the potential consequences of too much or too little trust?

Coalition-building requires a level of trust that we can describe as 'bounded' – we agree to trust each other in situations where our interests align.

Within a team, we can identify five levels of trust. The first is typical of a low psychologically safe environment and the fifth is typical of high psychological safety.

1 *Trust in self*: I trust myself more to get things done than I trust my colleagues.
2 *Task*: I trust my colleagues to do what they are supposed to.
3 *Conflict of ideas*: I can challenge opinions I don't agree with.
4 *Feelings*: I feel I can open up and be honest with my team colleagues about how I feel.
5 *Energy*: The level of trust we have is a core strength of this team.

Team coaching is an intervention that focuses on the building of trust as a foundation for improving collective performance and capability. The coaches help the team and its leader develop greater trust as part of building psychological safety. A starting point is often establishing team norms that set shared expectations of behaviours. These norms might, for example, look something like this:

- Suggestions are considered gratefully and not ridiculed.
- Criticism is given and received with goodwill – it's a sign of helpfulness.
- Everyone's contributions are valued.
- People with greater authority, experience or knowledge are open to new ideas and different perspectives.
- Naïve questions are seen as important in evaluating what the team is doing and why.
- Raising concerns will not result in being victimised or punished.
- The team are all committed to learning together.

Or maybe like this:

- We will not make assumptions about each other's motives or perspectives.
- We will listen with courtesy and respect.
- We will take joint ownership for the team's successes and failures.
- We will each present as our 'best person'.
- We will be generous towards each other.
- We will give each other the space to speak and ourselves the space to reflect.
- We will replace judgement with curiosity.

As the person (usually) with greatest authority in a team, the leader has a substantial influence on the level of psychological safety. The more they trust the team, the more the team members trust the leader and each other – and the higher the psychological safety. The key to building that trust lies initially in the leader's ability to demonstrate vulnerability. He or she can do this in many ways, such as asking the team for help, or seeking feedback from them around their personal and behavioural development plans. The leader also has an important role in protecting the team from external threats and interference, which can exacerbate fears.

Team coaches therefore work both with the team as a whole and with the leader, with the result that conversations between the team and the leader gradually become more authentic, more purposeful and more creative.

How the leader influences the team climate

Figure 5.1 illustrates the chain of effect when the leader exhibits both high emotional intelligence and self-security – and when he or she doesn't. In a study of high-performing teams in one of the world's largest technology companies, one of the key characteristics of those teams was the role and behaviour of the leader. Leaders of high-performing teams were secure in themselves. They had broad enough shoulders to take personal responsibility for failures and mistakes by team members. They did not seek to manage anyone – rather, they created an environment where people could manage themselves. They didn't want to be informed of everything – they trusted the team to tell them what they needed to know, in good time. They sought feedback from their teams about how they were helping and hindering. They protected the team from external interference (and particularly from external politics). They showed in multiple small ways that they cared both about the team purpose and about the team members. They also saw themselves as 'work in progress' – far from perfect and with a lot to learn.

Figure 5.1 Relationship between emotional intelligence and politics.

Ineffective leaders come in many shapes and sizes. At one extreme are the high narcissists and sociopaths. The latter, in particular, often come with malevolent intent. There's not a lot to be done with such leaders, other than seek to align their narrow, egotistical objectives with bigger, more desirable collective causes. Most ineffective leaders, however, are well-meaning people out of their depth. Their fear of being exposed leads them to try to control more and more and to employ more and more political ploys – which eventually make things worse. This behaviour is often referred to as *imposter syndrome*.

Imposter syndrome affects 70% of adults at some point in their careers. (Multiple studies arrive at different statistics, from 50% to 85%. Seventy per cent is a widely accepted figure, but much depends on research design and the circumstances of respondents.) Originally associated mostly with women in senior positions, when it was identified in the late 1970s, in reality it affects both genders. According to the California Institute of Technology Counseling Center, imposter syndrome is 'a collection of feelings of inadequacy that persist even in face of information that indicates that the opposite is true ... experienced internally as chronic self-doubt, and feelings of intellectual fraudulence'.

Imposter syndrome typically affects people when they have worked hard to achieve a new role or responsibility. Even though other people tell them they are doing well, they are constantly in fear of being 'found out' as not up to the task, or not deserving to be in the role. They feel as if they have been faking it and the more praise they receive, the less deserving they feel. To some extent, these reactions may be the result of an increased sense of responsibility – the more successful you are, the more responsibility you acquire and the greater the consequences of getting things wrong.

Men and women tend to respond differently to these feelings. Men tend to avoid situations where they might be exposed; women tend to put in more and more effort to live up to expectations.

Coaches and mentors can help clients overcome imposter syndrome in a variety of ways, including:

- Naming it. Describing what is happening as imposter syndrome helps to normalise it and make it less fearsome.
- Encouraging them not to take themselves too seriously. It's about achieving a balance between not taking any credit for your success and seeing yourself as more important than you really are.
- Exploring who they compare themselves with and how. What self-doubts do they think that person might have?
- Helping them see themselves as a work in progress and their job role as an ongoing experiment, in which getting some things wrong is an important part of the normal process. A great coaching question is: 'How many mistakes do you need to make each week to learn at the pace you need?'
- Exploring the impact of their negative self-beliefs on others. If, for example, they lead them to overmanage their direct reports, what would be the impact on team performance of a more relaxed approach trusting both oneself and one's team?
- Helping them practise vulnerability – for example, admitting what they don't know, talking about what they have learned from their mistakes. Imposter

syndrome pushes you to avoid vulnerability but having the courage to be *more* vulnerable gradually increases self-belief.

- Putting 'expertise' into context for them. An expert is someone whose great knowledge gets in the way of their learning. Instead of seeking to be an expert, it is better to be an enthusiastic learner.
- Getting them to have conversations between their confident and self-doubting selves. Choosing which self to step into (even if it feels like faking it to go with the confident self) provides a sense of control and goes a long way towards making the confident self the default self.
- Helping them set positive (towards) goals for their behaviour and thinking rather than negative (avoidance) goals. Negative goals simply remind them of their perceived inadequacies.
- Encouraging them to value their self-doubts as a stimulus for action – so, for example, preparing thoroughly for a presentation becomes less a matter of preventing any mistakes than of being the best they can.
- Sharing what you value in them, as a dispassionate external observer, who can provide a balanced perspective.

Further reading on this topic is provided at the end of the chapter.

The idea that there might be also an upside to imposter syndrome arose for us from two sources simultaneously. The first was a discussion during coach supervision of the role of self-doubt in how coaches approach assignments. Having what we might call *balanced self-doubt* keeps coaches on their toes and constantly curious.

The second source was a short section in the book *Think Again* by Adam Grant, who points to studies that suggest a strong positive link between performance and self-doubt. He outlines three key benefits of self-doubt:

- It makes us work harder and avoid complacency.
- It makes us work smarter, by prompting us to rethink our strategy.
- It makes us better learners, by seeking support and ideas from other people.

On the other hand, there is plenty of evidence that dysfunctional reactions to self-doubt lead us to:

- micro-manage in vain hopes of asserting control over outcomes
- work less smart, because we are afraid to admit our fears and weaknesses
- learn less, because we are afraid to ask for help.

The four Cs of great leaders and great coaches – Compassion, Courage, Curiosity and Connectedness – have a role here. Having compassion for ourselves gives us freedom to be wrong. It takes courage to ask for help and curiosity to seek better ways of doing things. And it takes connectedness to build around us a support network of people, who will give us both honest feedback and guidance.

So, what does it take for leaders, coaches and mentors to achieve balanced self-doubt? Some useful questions to ask in our reflections before and after coaching sessions include:

- What am I in danger of becoming complacent about?
- What assumptions about myself have I not challenged for a while?
- How can I increase my self-compassion and be kinder to myself?
- What conversations could I usefully have with my idealised self?
- How effective am I at using self-doubt to stimulate continuous learning?
- What would help me feel a great sense of 'I belong here'?
- How can I cultivate and nurture my network of collegial support?
- How will I know when I have a reasonable balance between complacency-arrogance and self-doubting humility?
- What experiments are waiting for me to try out, for my benefit and that of others?
- Where is the laughter in the system that is me and my professional role?

How the coach can help the leader overcome fear and build a psychological safe environment: a case study

The new divisional director came with a track record of getting things done, often over a trail of 'dead bodies'. His self-image was one of being driven, goal-focused yet human and caring. When he was accused of bullying, he was appalled. 'It's just an excuse for not doing their job.' A psychological safety questionnaire revealed that there were deep problems within his team, in terms of speaking up. When he insisted that he wanted to be challenged more, they didn't believe him, especially when he shot down a suggestion from one of them describing it as half-baked. Yet he still wouldn't accept he needed to change his behaviour. 'Let's try an experiment,' said the coach. 'Tell the team that at the next meeting, you are going to show them the difference between bullying and enthusiastic encouragement. Start with what it would be like to take a bullying approach.' With everyone's assent, the leader took one item on the agenda and demonstrated a bunch of bullying behaviours – for example, cutting people off, or being sarcastic. As guided by the coach beforehand, he watched the faces of his colleagues closely. After a few minutes, he paused and asked for a moment's silence. 'OK. I can't see much difference either. I need your help.' Game over!

The critical question in helping a leader who wants to build a different, supportive and safe environment in their team is 'What needs to happen for you to be your authentic self, 100% of the time?' Frequently, this leads to an exploration of 'Who is your authentic self?' If people have been acting out a role embedded in fear and anxiety, they may need first to rediscover and reconnect with their authentic self. Until they do that, they will struggle to help others feel safe.

Another key step is, 'How will you show your authentic self to your team?' Part of this involves the setting of group norms and committing to be the role model for those norms. Then, to create opportunities for the team to give feedback on how good a role model you are presenting.

The role of the coach is to support the leader through these reflections, rehearse difficult conversations and help the leader develop their compassion, courage, curiosity and connectedness. The role is also to help the leader develop their ability to work positively with politics, both inside the team and externally.

How the coach can help the team build greater psychological safety

Team coaches in particular have a substantial toolkit of approaches to help teams gradually develop psychological safety. A favourite technique in team coaching asks everyone to write on cards, in capital letters (to preserve anonymity), issues that no-one speaks about. The cards are gathered in, then redistributed randomly. Each team member in turn presents the issue on their card as if it were their own. Because no-one knows who brought the topic up, the presenter does not feel under pressure. The cat is out of the bag and there is no-one to blame! As the team develops more confidence in raising sensitive issues, when the exercise is repeated, more issues surface than at first. This is a great sign of increased psychological safety.

Another technique is to give everyone a bunch of envelopes with the names of their colleagues on each. They put into each envelope a note describing 'One thing I am going to do to make your life easier over the next month'. At the end of the month, they open the envelopes together. The effect of the exercise is felt in the switch of attention towards positive things team members do to support each other.

Surveying the team about the level of psychological safety can also be cathartic. The psychological safety questionnaire from Coaching and Mentoring International contains 20 questions that provide deep insights. For example:

- In the past month, I have pretended I understood something I really didn't.
- In the past month, I have been made to feel isolated or disloyal when I questioned something outside my area.

- It's not a good idea to question what the leader says.
- People say what they think others want to hear, not what they really think.

Psychological safety and team political awareness

While a team may rely on the leader to protect them from the worst of corporate politics emanating from outside the team, political naivety on the part of team members can undermine psychological safety and team performance. An example is a team in a small company recently acquired by a multinational giant. The team saw the acquisition as a great opportunity to develop new products they had been talking about for some time. They spent weeks preparing the business case for investment, doing initial product design and creating marketing plans. They put together what they thought was a powerful presentation and submitted it.

For three months nothing happened. Then a virtual meeting with one of the senior executives in the multinational headquarters explained the politics. 'These are great ideas and probably very viable. But they are too small. Nobody here at HQ is going to take any notice of any idea that promises less than $10 million annual profit. It's not worth the trouble!' Sometimes, the difference between organisational politics and internal marketing is very small!

Team coaching raises the collective awareness of the systems that impact the team and of which the team is a part by, for example, exploring the motivations and needs of stakeholders and the interactions between stakeholders. In a politically savvy team, everyone builds support networks they can use to hear about disruptive change informally, before key decisions out of their control are made. The 'politics of the possible' appear on the regular meeting agendas. Team members actively promote coalitions with peers in other teams, creating communities of influence outside the formal hierarchy.

'Let's talk about the political realities here' should not be something heard only at the most senior levels in an organisation. Whenever a team aims to maximise its contribution, there are three questions to consider:

- What influence do we need to bring to bear to achieve our objectives and purpose?
- What influence do we have?
- How will we acquire and/or exercise that influence?

When and how to speak up

Table 5.2 describes some of the common situations that occur in the workplace. In each case, an effective response demands emotional regulation – recognising the instinctive, naïve response, collecting oneself and then taking an approach that is both authentic and politically astute.

Table 5.2 Responding to common situations that occur in the workplace

Type of political challenge	Situation	Politically naïve	Politically astute
Conflicting agendas	Your colleague gives a presentation that has a hidden agenda	You don't notice You do notice and challenge them – and both of you are embarrassed	You play 'Devil's advocate' to clarify what is proposed – and hence reveal the flaws and hidden agenda. You defer a decision for further consultation, giving you an opportunity to marshal opposition
Selective with information	Your leader asks you to sugar-coat or manipulate information to 'keep face' instead of admitting he made a mistake	You refuse and threaten to resign	You say, 'Let's be creative about this. How can we turn it to our advantage?'
Access to information	Your leader excludes you from key stakeholder meetings and is selective with the information they share	You go behind their back	You respond to queries with 'I'm sorry; I'm not privy to that information'
Sharing information	Your colleague is withholding and hoarding information for a project you've taken over	You go up the chain and complain	You send a memo to key stakeholders along the lines of: 'These are the inherited problems I have been able to identify so far …'. In order to save face the colleague has to collaborate
Advantageous relationships	Your colleague is favoured for a piece of work, receiving preferential treatment for being the boss's pet	You complain to peers about how unfair it is	You build strong relationships with your boss's boss and his or her peers. You engage positively with your own boss and demonstrate your commitment and abilities

(continued)

Table 5.2 (continued)

Type of political challenge	Situation	Politically naïve	Politically astute
Speaking openly	You disagree with your leader's decision and are not sure how to raise it	You argue with them or suffer in silence	You ask them to work through their reasoning with you in private, so you can at least explain it to others. If you think it's all going to end badly, you plan ahead to how you will help your boss dig themselves out of the hole they have created
Recognition	Your leader is quick to dismiss your ideas and discourages your participation in senior meetings	It's not fair!	Find a sponsor at a more senior level and use them as a sounding board for your ideas before you go public with them. Make a point of publicly acknowledging the sponsor's contribution. Now it's much harder for your boss to steal the credit
Lack of fair treatment	You have been passed over for a promotion and feel unfairly rewarded for your good work	It's all their fault	It's up to me to manage my reputation better

References

Edmondson, A. (2019) *The Fearless Organization*. Hoboken, NJ: Wiley.

Grant, A. (2013) Rocking the boat but keeping it steady: The role of emotion regulation in employee voice, *Academy of Management Review*, 56 (6): 1703–1723.

Kahn, W.A. (1990) Psychological conditions of personal engagement and disengagement at work, *Academy of Management Journal*, 33 (4): 692–724.

Kish-Gephart, J.J., Detert, J.R., Treviño, L.K. and Edmondson, A.C. (2009) Silenced by fear: The nature, sources, and consequences of fear at work, in B.M. Staw and A.P. Brief (eds) *Research in Organizational Behavior*, volume 29. Greenwich, CT: JAI Press (pp. 163–193).

Milliken, F.J., Morrison, E.W. and Hewlin, P.F. (2003) An exploratory study of employee silence: Issues that employees don't communicate upward and why, *Journal of Management Studies*, 40 (6): 1453–1476.

Turner, T. (2019) *Teaming and Psychological Safety*, Australian Tax Office, Sydney, NSW, 9 August.

Further reading

Canning, E.A., LaCosse, J. and Kroeper, K.M. (2019) Feeling like an imposter: The effect of perceived classroom competition on the daily psychological experiences of first-generation college students, *Social Psychology and Personality Science*, 11 (5): 647–657.

Clance, P.R. and Ament, S. (1978) The impostor phenomenon among high achieving women: Dynamics and therapeutic intervention, *Psychotherapy, Research and Practice*, 15 (3): 241–247.

Cokley, K., Smith, L., Bernard, D., Hurst, A., Jackson, S., Stone, S., Awosogba, O., Saucer, C., Bailey, M. and Roberts, D. (2017) Impostor feelings as a moderator and mediator of the relationship between perceived discrimination and mental health among racial/ethnic minority college students, *Journal of Counseling Psychology*, 64 (2): 141–154.

Grant, A. (2021) *Think Again*. London: Penguin Random House.

Langford, J. and Clance, P.R. (1993) The impostor phenomenon: Recent research findings regarding dynamics, personality and family patterns and their implications for treatment, *Psychotherapy: Theory, Research, Practice, Training*, 30 (3): 495–501.

Muradoglu, M., Horne, Z., Hammond, M.D., Leslie, S.-J. and Cimpian, A. (2021) Women – particularly underrepresented minority women – and early-career academics feel like impostors in fields that value brilliance, *Journal of Educational Psychology*, 114 (5): 1086–1100.

Pedler, M. (2011) Leadership, risk and the imposter syndrome, *Action Learning: Research and Practice*, 8 (2): 89–91.

6 Gender, politics of privilege

Lise Lewis

Despite social pressures to reduce gender inequality, there remains an imbalance in how gender differences are perceived. Take this particularly inflammatory edict reported by Brinlee (2017):

> *Of course women must earn less than men because they are weaker, they are smaller, they are less intelligent, they must earn less, that's all.*
> – Janusz Korwin-Mikke, Polish politician and member of the European Parliament, 2017)

Let's recognise that both women and men are subject to both implicit and explicit inequality arising from organisational politics. Although generally, opinion seems to infer that women are more impacted despite the implementation of equality and inclusion legislation along with diversity policies into employment practices. We know these measures are only part of the equation to winning hearts and minds for the radical change anticipated. 'If gender discrimination is allowed to continue, the toxicity and dissatisfaction hurt the company's bottom line. Workplace performance eventually falls, and the organisation's integrity is compromised' (Robinson, 2021). With this reinforcement of the business case for transformational change, what can we learn from those at the sharp end of organisational politics?

This chapter draws on the primary research study informing this text and combines the findings from one-to-one 60-minute meetings with four of the nine women interviewed (word count restricted data input) and a group meeting with three men. The extended meetings with women gave voice to the apparent gender imbalance for engaging with organisational politics alongside an observation that women have a sense of being underprivileged when excluded by male-dominated leadership. Quotes expressing individual realities are cited as insights into how interviewees perceive being accepted or not, within organisational cultural norms, both tacit and espoused. The focus here is not to attempt to find solutions to what emerges in such complex issues, but rather to highlight the challenges faced through gender and how these feed privilege. I add personal reflections in places where memories are awakened whilst writing. These serve as reminders to us all of the emotional imprint that is sustained for those detrimentally affected by the negative side of organisational politics. I invite you to reflect on whether the findings resonate and whether you wish to settle for the status quo as being the 'way of the world' or you feel energised to disrupt and be an agent and role model for change. The aim here is to be a fellow traveller on that journey.

Attempts are made to offer a balanced view of gender and privilege in this chapter and where imbalance prevails, this mirrors what contributors see as their reality rather than authoring licence. The term 'coach' is used here to include coaches, mentors and coach supervisors.

As you read, you may like to think about how you view your role in similar scenarios to those illustrated. You may also like to review your behaviour within an organisational political framework when answering the following questions:

- What does it feel like to be 'a member of the tribe at work' despite wider society sometimes operating exclusion zones of acceptability in similar circumstances?
- How do you deal with feeling 'unaccepted at work', although the unacceptance is camouflaged by a glossy pretence of 'inclusion' denying an underbelly of organisational pretence?
- When do you find yourself avoiding recognition of overt unfair practices demeaning others in fear of repercussions for challenging?
- When do you engage with playing political games that undermine others despite personal discomfort and driven by self-preservation?
- How do you or might you use and apply political strategies to explore best solutions for workplace dilemmas?

How gender in politics is likely to inform privilege

Men and women appear to view office politics and power dynamics differently. Men tend to talk about 'competition' as 'tools people use to win at work'. Women often see politics as 'influencing others' (Heath, 2017).

Think about organisational situations that are familiar. How important is the language we use in determining 'how political we are' and how does language illustrate this quote from Heath? Expanding the theme of gender differences in language use and imagining overhearing a corridor conversation, we may hear something similar to:

We're likely to have a battle on our hands to convince others of the importance of throwing our energy into making this project a success. It's no good hoping shareholders will follow our lead if we don't show we mean to beat the competition into submission. We must be clear about our plan demonstrating fortitude in placing us in prime position as the most serious contender.

I hear what you say and agree that we show a planned approach and wonder about everyone's acceptance of using a strategy that appears to diminish others. Perhaps we're better placed to show forecasting evidence that predicts how we can excel. Hopefully this invites shareholders to engage with the dialogue about the feasibility of our proposals. I think this more inclusive approach is likely to persuade the shareholders that we can be taken seriously with our bid.

We may be ambivalent or see the merits of each as a persuasive approach and acknowledge or disagree that language is a strong predictor of gender. Add to this tone and volume of voice and speculation on gender and strength of argument starts to favour a male voice. Men and women may have the same assertive behaviours but does this mean that each are similarly perceived when observing style of delivery? Strident women leaders such as Margaret Thatcher, a former UK Prime Minister, are often perceived as aggressive; Jacinda Ardern, previously Prime Minister of New Zealand, with a more collaborative, kinder and compassionate approach, is reported in press coverage as lacking the qualities expected of a role with this level of political profile. The question is, whose template and norms of leadership are we applying in making this speculation?

An ideal man is supposed to be aggressive, ambitious, dominant, self-confident, and forceful, as well as self-reliant and individualistic. The takeaway: Being a good man and a good leader are one and the same. (Vanek Smith, 2021: 21)

Evidently, there is a ratio of 6:1 of a man's voice being 'heard' before that of a female (Sieghart, 2021). This text highlights both conscious and unconscious bias applied to women and detects a startling perspective that reveals the scale of the gap that still exists between men and women.

Sieghart invites the male reader to imagine:

- Having your views ignored or your expertise frequently challenged by women.
- Trying to speak up in a meeting only to be talked over by female colleagues.
- Direct reports resisting you as a boss, merely because you're a man.
- People always addressing the woman you are with before you.

What a graphic example this is of privilege based on gender alone. What a sad indictment demonstrating how organisations may be functioning with less than a full capacity of utilised talent – that of overlooking the worth of women's capability.

As a female representing one dimension of underprivilege, I'm shocked when sharing this quote from Sieghart to remember the frequency of when I've left unchallenged the inference made by this type of male behaviour. I recall commenting or sharing a view at meetings without receiving acknowledgement of my speaking and without any response. This left me wondering if what I was saying was total nonsense, or perhaps more generously I hadn't expressed my thoughts in an understandable way – or even having a low timbre to my voice, maybe I hadn't been heard. That is until I hear the same thoughts expressed in a slightly different format by a man congratulated for offering a great idea! What I notice as I share this event is adopting the common female stance of first taking responsibility for how others react.

Frankly, I've lost count of the number of times that men have spoken over me and drowned out my voice. Maturity has offered the space to speak out when interrupted and recently I appreciated an email 'apologising profusely', to use his words, when challenging what was evidently an unintended interruption. Perhaps an unconscious reflexive action on his part? We can all become excited in the moment about a perceived great idea and be over-enthusiastic in gauging appropriate timing for sharing. This can inadvertently or perhaps intentionally prompt speaking over others. The abundance of incidents lacking understandable 'enthusiastic energy' can only be recognised as a wish to be heard and perhaps prevent making space for others' opinions.

These intrusions left me feeling 'invisible', disrespected and perceived as lacking the ability to make worthwhile contributions. I want to believe that the actions generating these reactions are driven by unconscious bias. Sadly, I'm far from alone as the sample from the primary and secondary research findings illustrates later in this chapter, offering evidence of privilege assumed or bestowed based on gender learned expectations.

Applying this type of gender privilege into organisational politics in its widest definition represents part of the informal system from which 'outsiders' are excluded. An interviewee in the secondary research described this as the 'inner circle'. She knew who was in the inner circle and she felt she could gain access. However, she also realised 'how quickly she could be trampled to death' in the inner circle. She didn't want to be in the outer circle though, as this meant she wouldn't know 'what was going on in the closed agenda' (inner circle) and preferred to stay in the 'middle circle' where she gains a sense of both the open agenda and what and who was helpful to maintain alliances with. Here we start to reveal a sense of how political activity is also linked with 'power'. Who has power and who doesn't and what privileges are adopted by or bestowed upon anyone adept at playing the political game?

Political norms determine how power can be achieved, used and what needs to happen to sustain the gifts that power brings. Think of the employee who becomes the expert networker, knows the person you need to talk with when seeking 'insider' knowledge, is someone who is popular, liked by everyone and seems to progress in the organisation with apparent ease and without too much evidence of role achievement. How does this person present to you? Well deserving of this level of recognition gained from being adept at leveraging political acumen or someone perceived as gaining unfair advantage over others who are accepted as 'hard workers' lacking recognition: those who keep their 'heads down' and just get on with their work?

Questions to ask ourselves might be about what this lens is revealing for us about power and how our reflections on these questions inform and guide future intentions:

- Who has the power in working relationships?
- Who is perceived as having power?
- Who wants power?
- How do we relate to the power these people appear to own?
- What impact do they have on us?
- What level of personal power do we have?
- How is this recognised by others?

Although men hold the majority of top leadership positions, studies recognise that women have the attributes to effectively lead. Chamorro-Premuzic and Gallop (2020) suggest that rather than 'advising female executives to act more like men to get ahead, society would be better served by more male leaders trying to emulate women'. They offer seven attributes that men can learn from women:

1 Don't grab opportunities without the talent to back them up
2 Know your own limitations
3 Motivate through transformation
4 Put your people ahead of yourself
5 Don't command; empathise
6 Focus on elevating others
7 Be humble.

Thematic analysis of gender issues: primary research

In Chapter 1, we provide an overview of survey findings inviting the views of business leaders, coaches, mentors and supervisors. Analysis of this primary research data identifies a range of influences affecting gender issues in organisations.

The global gender mix distribution of those completing the survey questionnaires is shown in Figure 6.1. This pie chart infers that the responses in Table 6.1 are slightly more significant for female responders and also acknowledges that the measures are representative of the questionnaire as a whole and not directly attributable to individual questions.

Figure 6.1 Survey responses by gender.

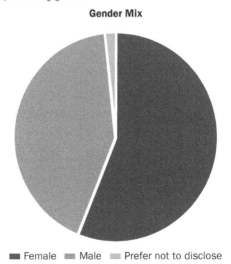

Gender Mix

■ Female ■ Male ▨ Prefer not to disclose

Table 6.1 Thematic analysis extract from primary research

Column 1: Thematic analysis of questionnaire responses	**Column 2:** Response indicators suggesting a political context of survey findings	**Column 3:** Response indicators suggesting the typical Impact of survey findings

Part A. ENABLERS: POSITIVE INFLUENCES attributable to organisational politics

Themes	Organisational political context	POSITIVE influence
Equality, Diversity, Inclusivity, Collaboration	• Fairness and a sense of equity • Fosters and values diversity • Understands individual values and concerns • Enables co-creation • Robust debate • Adopts a systemic approach exposing a wider range of perspectives and experiences • Cultural collaboration • Inclusive and empowering • Confronts and manages unconscious bias related to gender, culture, ethnicity, etc. • Encourages progression • Favours synergies, alignment and new possibilities • Embraces diversity of views • Encourages autonomy	• Validation for employees • Unlocks full potential of the organisation • Accesses collective wisdom • Allows more creativity and experimentation • Strong team cohesion • Enhanced job satisfaction • Sense of empowerment • Increased ownership and accountability

Part B. DISABLERS: NEGATIVE INFLUENCES attributable to organisational politics

Themes	Organisational political context	NEGATIVE influence
Damaging Behaviours	• Unfair and unsaid (although perceived) biases based on relationships and allegiances • 'Survival of the fittest' actions • Toxic, narcissistic power games • Simultaneously backstabbing with a smile • Advances own agenda	• Inequality • Unfairness • Undermines performance • Detrimental to wellbeing • Inability to be honest • Feeling silenced • Lack of transparency and openness • Self-preservation

(continued)

Table 6.1 (*continued*)

Part B. DISABLERS: NEGATIVE INFLUENCES attributable to organisational politics

Themes	Organisational political context	NEGATIVE influence
Navigating Biases	• Unfair treatment – disproportionate reward system • Individual agendas driving decisions • Lack of opportunity/support • Unfair system • Ungracious feedback • Unfairness in promotions • Issues of recognition and pay • Gender discrimination • Leaders embarrass/demean when perceived as overstepping • Favouritism • Lack of transparent dialogue • Personal income and social protections • Fairness in promotions • Reduction in working hours while maintaining same salary • Promotions for some without achieving goals • Patriarchy 'won't let women in' • Taking undue credit for work • Leaders perceived 'not to walk the talk'	• Need to be recognised and navigated • Frustrations with procedures • Jealousy • Resentment • Demotivation • Withdrawal from leadership roles and commitment when unequally rewarded compared with less qualified leaders • Feelings of an unfair system • Lack of innovation • Teams are left short-staffed

Part C. NEGATIVE/POSITIVE INFLUENCES attributable to organisational politics

Themes	Negative disablers attributable to organisational politics	Positive enablers attributable to organisational politics
Use of Power	• Power plays/games • Enhances own power • Establishes power dynamics that sustain power, rank and privilege • Acquires or shares status • Uses covert/overt power to reach objectives	• Uses power to attain desired outcomes • Decisions influenced by power • Stays close to the 'power group'

Table 6.1 uses the thematic analysis (Column 1) extracted from the primary research responses aligned with the political context (Columns 2 for Parts A and B) to demonstrate the enablers (positive influences) and disablers (negative influences) attributable to organisational politics (Column 3). Part C demonstrates the impact of organisational politics generating both disablers (Column 2: negative influences) and enablers (Column 3: positive influences) for the theme of 'Use of Power' (Column 1).

This extract of primary survey findings suggests that:

- Recognising and addressing the negative impact of equality, diversity and inclusivity issues are a positive influencer and invite and support collaboration.
- Accommodating damaging behaviours and tolerating bias disenfranchise and have a negative and disempowering effect on those impacted.
- Use of power can accommodate both negative and positive influences depending on intention.

Thematic analysis of gender issues: secondary research

Sixty-minute interviews with a sample of nine women specifically discussed gender issues. The interviews encouraged a conversational approach based loosely on the primary survey questionnaire circulated in advance and depending on whether the interviewees perceived themselves as a leader, coach, mentor or supervisor. Additional comments were collected from three men responding to the general question of how gender issues were perceived within an organisational political context.

Comparison between primary and secondary indicators specific to gender

Table 6.2 replicates (Column 1) the responses extracted from the primary research (in Table 6.1) suggesting the typical impact of organisational politics. Column 2 represents verbatim comments from secondary research participants illustrating perceptions of the impact of organisational politics.

Table 6.2 Responses from secondary research aligned with themes from primary research

Column 1: PRIMARY: Response indicators suggesting a typical impact	**Column 2:** SECONDARY: Verbatim indicators from secondary research endorsing individual perceptions of experiencing and managing organisational politics
Part A. ENABLERS: POSITIVE INFLUENCES	
• Validation for employees • Unlocks full potential of the organisation • Accesses collective wisdom • Allows more creativity and experimentation • Strong team cohesion • Enhanced job satisfaction • Sense of empowerment • Increased ownership and accountability	• They are part of the culture, although you can't see them clearly; they're used like self-serving behaviours and involve the use of power and social networking • I think politics give order • Create energy for change; use internal politics by socialising ideas, getting to people and finding out who the powerful people are, and making sure you know they're on your side before going into a formal meeting • Create consensus behind what you think is the right action … compromise when you think you're swimming against the flow • It's no good us thinking and making the assumption that all men are political when we're talking about gender • Don't be afraid of politics and use it with positive intent; internal and cross-organisational politics can actually be a really helpful tool in levering change
Part B. DISABLERS: NEGATIVE INFLUENCES	
• Inequality • Unfairness • Undermines performance • Detrimental to wellbeing • Inability to be honest • Feeling silenced • Lack of transparency and openness • Self-preservation • Need to be recognised and navigated • Frustrations with procedures • Jealousy	• Politics has no place in organisations as it prevents people from being authentic and violates individual values • Being transparent and fair is naïve and unrealistic • Individuals have to fit with the 'company profile', which undermines diversity and inclusion, encouraging different people with different opinions • It's difficult for women to use their feminine power, intelligence or attributes that could benefit the company • We are losing honesty because we have to be 'politically correct' and it's difficult to understand perspectives in every culture.

Table 6.2 (*continued*)

Column 1: PRIMARY: Response indicators suggesting a typical impact	**Column 2:** SECONDARY: Verbatim indicators from secondary research endorsing individual perceptions of experiencing and managing organisational politics
• Resentment • Demotivation • Withdrawal from leadership roles and commitment when unequally rewarded in comparison to less qualified leaders • Feelings of an unfair system • Lack of innovation • Teams are left short-staffed	• He was like a chameleon saying whatever he thought people wanted to hear and moved from meeting to meeting saying the exact opposite • The only way I could take control was to get out of this situation (and to leave) • I realised how quickly I could be 'trampled to death' in the inner circle – I gave up some of my moral values by doing this as I wasn't speaking out • People who want to be true to themselves and don't fit with the anticipated 'stereotypical norm' end up being penalised one way or another • My learning is you've got to be more active in neutralising people who are actively working against you • I wasn't feeling very resilient; even the people you think are on your side cannot be relied on for support when things get difficult • The organisation is male-dominated with male language and norms carried into business meetings that excludes women • The learning about speaking out being less than well received was to 'wake up' and be aware of expected behaviour • There is very low psychological safety at senior level, so people have a fear of speaking up to avoid different opinions and disagreements • Ideas can be undermined if men feel threatened by a woman • I had quite a few experiences where a woman who wanted to be an alpha female was very threatened by other women who perhaps challenged her status

(*continued*)

Table 6.2 (*continued*)

Column 1: PRIMARY: Response indicators suggesting a typical impact	**Column 2:** SECONDARY: Verbatim indicators from secondary research endorsing individual perceptions of experiencing and managing organisational politics
	• If you're in a toxic system, then people who aren't necessarily bad people behave really badly and I think women are pushed to do that … push, push down of other women • 'Women who behave like men' aren't helpful (by emulating men's general behaviour as a role model for women) • I knew I was being excluded and things were done behind my back. It makes me feel sad to play the game to get the result needed for the company

Part C. DISABLERS/ENABLERS: NEGATIVE/POSITIVE INFLUENCES

• Uses power to attain desired outcomes • Decisions influenced by power • Stay close to the 'power group'	*DISABLERS*: • Is it ever a good thing if the person holding the power has good ideas – can the organisational politics be used for good – as it's usually used for bad, isn't it? • Power is held by a very small group • I was asked to do something that 'crossed the line' which didn't sit well with me • I trusted people I shouldn't have trusted, so it becomes a spiral going from being fierce in a positive way in terms of calling it out and feeling awful to feeling powerless *ENABLERS*: • Societal norms relating to gender need challenging so that both men and women are treated fairly • I think there are massive benefits to being 'politically astute'; it's about using the hidden dynamics in the organisation and using power. You can either use that negatively for self-interest or in a positive way • You need to be in a position of power to call it out

Extracting a few comments from Table 6.2 demonstrates a mix of experiences and ways of managing organisational politics.

Potential for change:

- 'The organisation is male-dominated with male language and norms carried into business meetings that excludes women' draws a strong gender boundary reinforcing what appears to be an unsurpassable division between men and women to the point of female exclusion.
- 'Ideas can be undermined if men feel threatened by a woman' is clearly discriminatory and begs the question about the insecurities driving the protection of male self-esteem.
- 'There is very low psychological safety at senior level, so people have a fear of speaking up to avoid different opinions and disagreements': a gender-free statement masking what was described elsewhere in the interview as male-dominated at senior level illustrates more about the individual than the gender.

Encouraging change:

- 'Create energy for change; use internal politics by socialising ideas, getting to people and finding out who the powerful people are, and making sure you know they're on your side before going into a formal meeting': intended as a positive 'makes sense' strategy by embracing organisational politics, although those with a dislike for politics may see this approach as massaging outcomes?
- 'Don't be afraid of politics and use it with positive intent; internal and cross-organisational politics can actually be a really helpful tool in levering change': an acceptance that organisational politics exists and if used purposefully can achieve productive advantage.

Responses from a 'speed survey' with three males

A meeting inviting attendees to 'check in' gave an opportunity to briefly introduce this topic and to ask a group of three men: *'How do you perceive gender issues in an organisational context?'*

Respondent A immediately responded, 'I can't see the problem!'
This statement was uttered as an exclamation and delivered with what appeared as a wry smile. My internal female reflexive response was 'this topic is not being taken seriously and implicitly appears to be declaring a position of one-upmanship': interesting to observe 'man' appearing in one-upmanship. Result: a sensation of 'power over': stimulating a sensation of the man positioning himself as dominant. A script that can automatically be ascribed in this situation is 'I wonder if he realises that he's declaring what appears to be male supremacy over women?' A surprising

reaction knowing this person; or was my assumption generated by learned past experiences being triggered and transferred?

Another interpretation can be 'he's just being playful', although there is a darker side to these 'games that people play' that again can typify 'power over'. The lingering question is, can this be unconscious defensive reflexivity emerging in response to male reactions, or is power being used disrespectfully and possibly unconsciously? Is this the kind of exchange condoned as acceptable workplace banter?

Respondent B offered a more reflective response: 'The question is dependent on the cultural perspective.'
He continued: 'I know senior executives who are terrified of women especially when they are attractive and aged mid-forties. There can be an unconscious discomfort reminiscent of relationships with mothers and/or wives; all the women who have rejected men; this is not to perceive this as bad – just the reality.'

B recalled a CFO coaching client, who was perceived as being 'armoured' with professional standards. The brief was 'we just need her to relax'. Women were seen as over-performing by establishing standards and how they felt about themselves when aspiring to 'be perfect'. The male lens was – what does it take for a female to relax – without questioning the legitimacy of 'over-performing'? The emphasis for coaching was the female being encouraged 'to pause' and 'to relax' to reduce the inner tension driven by expecting unnecessary high standards.

The question remains, who needs to change here?

- the woman striving to improve, or
- the male sponsor deciding the woman's aspirations for raising standards needed diluting, or
- the male coach?

As is the nature of shared coaching conversations, what was actually said in the session remains the domain of the people present. Maybe the woman was striving for unattainable perfection, although I have to empathise with her for being apparently criticised for wanting to encourage and deliver good performance. I can't help visualising how she must have felt deflated at least with having her well-intentioned efforts diminished. As can often happen, it can be the sponsor who will benefit from coaching; what did he anticipate would be the impact on employee morale and business performance with having a focus on reducing standards?

I believe coach B's intention was to be a positive enabler of change that would support this woman to be more aligned with business expectations. Unconscious bias prompted by social conditioning may have encouraged acceptance of the coaching assignment from a male leader, preventing questioning the sponsor's rationale for encouraging reducing standards.

Respondent C expanded the dialogue to include the perspective of sexuality within an organisational context.

C's experience as a gay man illustrated that once this was known he received an adverse reaction that overflowed into engagement with others. 'C' felt able to make comparisons with gender inequalities. He referred to how women leaders have to prove themselves and how women in his location have become VPs, although there was a 'long way to go' on gender. Power distribution was unequal with women having to 'fight' to gain personal power.

A sense of reciprocity flowed in this response with an empathy for mutual understanding.

Respondent A completed the sharing by adding to B's offering about how men relate to women.

'There is a disconnect when men have been rejected by women: they have difficulty seeing women as leaders. The solution is to coach the man to see this – not the woman – when a man has to prove himself – subconsciously there is a fear of being rejected which can be misinterpreted by women. Stress increases; this is transferred to the woman who unconsciously reacts by counter-transferring the behaviour anticipated by the man.'

The question here may be: are the complexities of relational dynamics an entry to unequal practices?

What we learn from the research findings

Comparing primary and secondary research responses suggests:

- Politics are accepted as part of organisational life; they may or may not be explicitly recognised.
- Political astuteness can be an enabler.
- Politics can be a positive force for engagement, facilitating change and reinforcing the psychological contract.
- Engaging with politics cannot be directly attributable to all males.
- Politics can have a negative influence on people's willingness to be authentic.
- Working within a defined political context can diminish the opportunity inherent in diverse thinking by discouraging honesty and access to different people with different opinions.
- Self-preservation can mean avoiding the political arena, including fitting with the 'stereotypical norm' and applying the ultimate surrender of leaving the organisation.
- Being caught up in a political melee intent on power often leads to feelings of being powerless.
- Diluting the impact of negative political activity is possible for those in 'power' positions.

An overview of the two research studies indicates that organisational politics can be beneficial and a useful resource when used purposefully and with positive intent. Alternatively, there are reflections of negativity in the context of gender-related issues, where politics appears to be an instrument of manipulation, used to access 'power over' positions and a means to gain advantage over another.

What are we prepared to influence?

Social rejection – or fearing it – is one of the most common causes of anxiety. Feelings of inclusion depend not so much on having frequent social contacts or numerous relationships as on how accepted we feel, even in just a few key relationships (Goleman, 2006). Reviewing again the statements offered from the research reminds us that the people energised to engage with the surveys want change. The message is clear – people are suffering with the detrimental impact of implicit or explicit damaging political discourse.

Maintaining the view that there is balance between 'good and bad', organisational politics remains easier for those benefiting from the positive effects. What becomes increasingly difficult is for those harmed by adverse political invective to adopt a similar perspective.

Becoming conscious of unconscious bias

Professor Joan Roughgarden of Stanford University states: 'Women are assumed to be incompetent unless proven otherwise, and men are assumed to be competent unless proven otherwise' (quoted by Sieghart, 2018). Sieghart (2021) suggests that 'confidence is so complicated for women and so uncomplicated for men'. We're reminded that when men are disproportionately seen in top positions, 'we are going to associate "male" with "leader", "success" and "competence" and "female" with "home", "children" and "family" [overriding] any natural bias women might have towards their own kind' (Sieghart, 2018).

So how does this bias manifest? This association between 'male' and 'leader' becomes lodged in the unconscious part of the brain creating bias towards women as leaders. As we're unaware of this unconscious phenomenon when asked to 'choose' who we believe is the most appropriate to lead – male or female – we choose the male. Combine this with recruiting people in our 'own likeness' and it's not surprising more men than women are employed as leaders.

Reducing the detrimental health effects of inappropriate organisational politics

Responding to the increase in mental health issues, wellbeing is gaining traction as an employee retention concept when the anxiety-inducing effects of Covid-19, environmental concerns and pace of change increase. Statistics offer insight into employers being aware of their responsibility and the business case for the physical, mental and social wellbeing of employees:

- 16% more productive, if satisfied with working environment
- 18% more likely to stay
- 30% more attracted to their company over competitors
- 66% more likely to accept a new job or keep the one they have in a workplace focused on their health and wellbeing (Meister, 2019).

The future is promoting happiness in employees – being more conscious of wellbeing – that will erode toxic politics. Although the intention of this chapter is to identify the influences rather than solutions for apparent gender inequality in business, both research studies suggest areas to be challenged. These questions remain:

- What appetite is there for change whether we're personally impacted or not?
- Are the findings recorded in this chapter sufficiently representative that to leave such practices unchallenged denies respect for humanity?
- How prepared are we to recognise or work on revealing our own personal biases and 'blind spots' to drive the change?
- What can we actively contribute to shifting the balance towards furthering 'good' and 'nurturing' political activities?
- What can we influence in the wider system to uncover power dynamics undermining healthy organisational practices?

These are questions for us to reflect on whatever our role and to be honest with ourselves about our responsibility to influence. I believe that advocating inclusivity deserves more sincerity of intention. If we truly want improvements and accept organisational politics as enabling, we must seek change, be open to encouraging and joining dialogue without recrimination, genuinely listen and be prepared to act and redress imbalances. Being human doesn't mean being equal; realistically this is unachievable. It does mean deserving of respect and care. Coaching has matured and has to be receptive to the complexity of practising at a deeper level for developing the wisdom that leaders need for the future of work.

Robinson (2021) suggests that minimising, covering up or turning your head the other way make the company become a revolving door for workers. Talented employees can always find a mentally healthier and more supportive work environment that makes accommodations for gender equality for all workers.

Silence condones acceptance of disadvantaging others!

We have choices about how we engage with organisational politics: to actively be in service of others and the business or to be disruptive for personal gain. The Influence Reservoir (Figure 6.2) symbolises an enabling container for coaching that invites leaders to role-model the positive features of organisational politics by leveraging:

- *Role status* to encourage and enable generative and productive practices.
- *Personal power* to champion inclusivity that celebrates everyone's unique talents.
- *Gender attributions* equalised as complementary and cooperatively more productive.
- *Distributed power* enabling and valuing contributions throughout the organisation.
- *Cultural mobility* that celebrates the richness of talent available in the global workplace and fairly recognises gender capability.

Figure 6.2 The Influence Reservoir

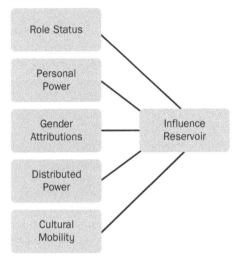

Emerson (2022) encourages us to seek out the distinction between ways that 'men and women work, communicate and lead [as being] a critical step in promoting and achieving gender parity'. It's only by integrating and encouraging these differences that we gain 'strength and flexibility to an organisation's leadership, and that diversity of thought can promote organisational success'.

The success of emerging women leaders depends heavily on the mid-level and senior managers (still predominantly white men) who are primarily responsible for their promotion. These senior managers can be instrumental in helping women to manage politics and to raise awareness amongst male leaders of how they can positively influence good practice and change malpractices that disadvantage women. Thus, mid-level and senior leaders have an active role to play in ensuring that emerging women have the same opportunities for advancement, promotion and career growth as their male co-workers.

Socialisation plays a huge part in 'dampening down' female willingness to self-promote and has been well publicised as a phenomenon that disables many women's enthusiasm to seek recognition by climbing the corporate ladder, let alone be involved in organisational politics as a way of influencing visibility. Women who want parity with men in the employment market are likely to have to change too.

Brené Brown (2018) has become well known for her campaign of distinguishing female leadership traits through being bold and willing to promote vulnerability as a leadership strength. She talks about 'daring leadership' to typify female traits. As you read the following, visualise the likely impact on organisational politics. What do you notice that may persuade acceptance of positive benefits for those who currently prefer to avoid engagement?:

- Modelling and encouraging healthy striving, empathy and self-compassion
- Practising gratitude and celebrating milestones and victories
- Setting boundaries and finding real comfort
- Making contributions and taking risks
- Knowing our value
- Cultivating commitment and shared purpose
- Straight talking and taking action
- Leading from heart.

Practices to encourage implementation of enabling practices

In summary, this chapter emphasises gender-based perceptions of organisational politics; the reality for women interviewed combined with impressions from literature and whether these views colour readiness to connect or provoke avoidance. Given the permanency of organisational politics as the informal conduit for 'lubricating whatever wheels those participating wish to turn', here are some suggestions for leaders and coaches to recognise and encourage to grow a fair and healthy political organisational culture:

Leadership:

- Role-model genuine authenticity that builds psychological safety and trust that ethical practices drive business performance.
- Introduce internal support networks sponsored by senior leadership inviting dialogue for change that manages expectations.
- Encourage attendance at external support networks to learn from and share good practice.

Coaching practice:

- Surfacing and replacing disabling societal norms and individual limiting beliefs with enabling ways of being.
- Challenging the concept that working harder gains recognition and encouraging visibility as a promotion influencer.

- Recognising and replacing language that diminishes accomplishments and disempowers self.
- Building self-esteem and confidence by recognising the true value of achievements.
- Working with clients to recognise the reality of boundaries excluding political engagement.
- Noticing and evaluating together the currency of 'alpha male' behaviours compared with alternative profiles that foster relational engagement, with clients behaving as 'traditional men' and believing this to be legitimate. In the extreme, is there potential for moving across a stepping stone path from:
  - misogyny
  - oblivion to the power imbalance (blissfully unaware)
  - recognising it although resistant to do anything about it
  - accepting that not addressing the issue is abuse of power
  - working to prevent this abuse of power
  - to work at creating and encouraging equal power?
- Being conscious of own gender as a potential powerful stimulus invoking strong reactions, if challenging perceptions about gender and encouraging behavioural change:
  - avoiding assumptions about the client's gender identity
  - being conscious of the influence of own gender
  - taking time to reveal the strength of recognisable gender bias before challenging the status quo
  - empathising without colluding and limiting self-disclosure.

References

Brinlee, M. (2017) 8 regressive quotes about women's rights from male politicians in 2017, *Bustle*, 20 May 20. Available at: https://www.bustle.com/p/8-regressive-quotes-about-womens-rights-from-male-politicians-in-2017-59199.

Brown, B. (2018) *Dare to Lead: Brave work. Tough conversations. Whole hearts.* London: Vermilion.

Chamorro-Premuzic, T. and Gallop C. (2020) 7 leadership lessons men can learn from women, *Harvard Business Review*, 1 April. Available at: https://hbr.org/2020/04/7-leadership-lessons-men-can-learn-from-women.

Emerson, M.S. (2022) The benefits of promoting gender diversity in leadership, *Professional Development, Harvard Division of Continuing Education* [blog], 7 January. Available at: https://professional.dce.harvard.edu/blog/benefits-of-promoting-gender-diversity-in-leadership/.

Goleman, D. (2006) *Social Intelligence: The new science of human relationships.* London: Hutchinson.

Heath, K. (2017) 3 simple ways for women to rethink office politics and wield more influence at work, *Harvard Business Review*, 18 December. Available at: https://hbr.org/2017/12/3-simple-ways-for-women-to-rethink-office-politics-and-wield-more-influence-at-work.

Meister, J.C. (2019) Survey: What employees want most from their workspaces, *Harvard Business Review*, 26 August. Available at: https://hbr.org/2019/08/survey-what-employees-want-most-from-their-workspaces.

Robinson, B. (2021) Gender discrimination is still alive and well in the workplace in 2021, *Forbes*, 15 February. Available at: https://www.forbes.com/sites/bryanrobinson/2021/02/15/gender-discrimination-is-still-alive-and-well-in-the-workplace-in-2021/.

Sieghart, M.A. (2018) Why are even women biased against women?, *Analysis*, BBC Radio 4. Available at: https://www.bbc.co.uk/programmes/articles/312fXcsr5T1V9p509XN-MYC4/why-are-even-women-biased-against-women.

Sieghart, M.A. (2021) *The Authority Gap: Why women are still taken less seriously than men, and what we can do about it*. London: Doubleday.

Vanek Smith, S. (2021) *Machiavelli for Women: Defend your worth, grow your ambition, and win the workplace*. New York: Gallery Books.

7 Developing social presence and authentic networking

David Clutterbuck and Tim Bright

This chapter explores the mechanisms by which people manage reputation and connection. Networking is by nature a political activity. We explore the reasons that people network and the concept of authentic reputation management within intelligent networking, drawing on current networking theory. We also explore the roles of coaches, mentors and sponsors as part of the social network that enables authentic reputation management.

Principles of authentic reputation management

As is so often the case, the Ancient Greeks had the concept of reputation management nailed down more than 2,000 years ago. Said Socrates: 'The way to gain a good reputation is to endeavour to be what you desire to appear.'

How we are perceived by others (or more accurately, how we believe we are perceived by others) shapes our identity – both internally and how we present ourselves to others. Most people (chronic sociopaths potentially excepted) want to be seen as 'good'. For example, a survey of prisoners in gaol revealed that the majority thought of themselves as more ethical than the 'average prisoner'. They perceived themselves to be more moral, kinder, more self-controlled, more compassionate, more generous, more dependable, more trustworthy and more honest. When asked how they compared themselves with the people at large, they rated themselves as equal to the average (Sedikides et al., 2014)!

In working with teams, we have found that a pragmatic way out of conflict between members is to ask questions, such as the following:

- What would your ideal self do right now?
- What would your kindest and most generous self want to say?
- What could we collectively say or do now that would bring out the best in each other?

- What gift can we extend to each other at this moment?
- What can we let go of now that will make us proud of ourselves later?

The power of these questions is that most people want to be authentic, most of the time. It is the pressure of the systems and situations we find ourselves in that causes us to be inauthentic (see Table 7.1). A common example of this is imposter syndrome, which we discussed in Chapter 5. As we stated there, our aim is to achieve balanced self-doubt and coaches need to apply the four Cs of great leaders and great coaches: Compassion, Courage, Curiosity and Connectedness. Having compassion for ourselves gives us freedom to be wrong. It takes courage to ask for help and curiosity to seek better ways of doing things. And it takes connectedness to build around us a support network of people, who will give us both honest feedback and guidance.

Table 7.1 Authentic and inauthentic reputation management

Inauthentic assumptions	Authentic assumptions
I have to be the person that others expect me to be	I try to be the person that I expect myself to be
I must pay a lot of attention to managing other people's perceptions of me	Time spent on managing other people's perceptions would be better spent on just being myself
I must conceal my fears and weaknesses	If I am open about my fears and weaknesses, other people will be supportive
I always carefully manage what I allow other people to see in me	If I act with integrity, other people are more likely to see me as I am
I take critical feedback as an attack on my person	I welcome critical feedback, because it helps me become closer to my ideal person
It's important to me to be liked by those people who can influence my career	It's important to me to be respected – and not just by those people who are influential
It's better to keep silent, when my views don't align with the majority view or the views of the most powerful people in the room	I add value by being the person who tests and questions the majority view
I sometimes have to hide my motivations	I try always to be open and honest about my motivations
I avoid thinking about the gap between my ideal self and my actual self	I talk with my ideal self as a friend, who helps me to grow

The value of reputation management

While it's hard to find concrete evidence, it's widely accepted that a gender difference in career self-management lies in the assumptions that men and women often make with regard to where reputation is built. It seems that women are more likely to assume that doing your job exceptionally well is the key to being noticed and given substantial developmental opportunities. Men, on the other hand, are more likely to assume that doing your job well is just a hygiene factor – it's what you do on top of your job (assuming that you do your job well) that gets noticed. Whether this gender difference is real or assumed isn't the issue, however. The critical factor is how much attention and energy you put into putting yourself forward for projects that have a wider influence, bring you into contact with decision-makers and influencers outside your normal circle, and allow you to prove that you can add value much more broadly. In a study David led for Kinsley Lord in the 1990s (Clutterbuck and Dearlove, 1995), we looked at career transitions and found that people most often got promoted when they were demonstrating that they were thinking and operating in ways that would be expected from someone at the next level of responsibility.

Reputation management, therefore, is about raising awareness of who you are and how you can contribute value – to immediate colleagues, to people who know you but not well and to people who do not yet know you at all. It's less about selling yourself than ensuring that, when people have a need for someone with your experience and talents, they know who to come to. There's a big mental gap between A: 'how can I make use of being connected with you?' and B: 'how can I help you?'. Authentic reputation management sits roughly in the middle of this spectrum (see Figure 7.1).

Where you, as a leader or as a coach, decide you want to be on this spectrum is totally up to you. Whether you are a leader or a coach, it depends ultimately on what you want to achieve. Take a look at the world's highest earning executive coaches, for example. (Or to be more accurate, those people describing themselves as executive coaches.) With few exceptions they are high narcissists with a heavy leaning towards the A side of the spectrum. Building high numbers of contacts and followers on social media is a means to making money and feeding an ego. If this sounds like 'buying reputation', sometimes it is just that. Now look at the coaches who have contributed most to knowledge in the field, to the social applications of coaching – and who are driven in large part by the potential for co-learning. They mostly fall into the B side of the spectrum. Of course, it's possible to move from one side to the other – and there are notable examples of this. But if you are a coach now, ask yourself honestly: 'Where do I fall?'

Figure 7.1 A spectrum of social-media-based reputation management.

Self-focused ————————————————— Other-focused

A   B

The value of authenticity

When people behave inauthentically, they are making a value judgement about the comparative virtues of authenticity and inauthenticity – usually in specific contexts. Those judgements may be skewed by greater attention to the fear of social punishment than to the positive benefits of being authentic. There may also be a timing issue – inauthentic compliance happens in the moment, while authenticity is the product of longer-term consistency of behaviour.

Various studies demonstrate correlations between authenticity in the workplace and general wellbeing (e.g. Toor and Ofori, 2009). Abigail Mengers (2014) found that being authentic was also associated with positive self-esteem that arises from a sense of being a unique individual. Standing out from the crowd (rather than blending in) for positive reasons is revealed as a form of self-affirmation.

There are different ways of understanding authenticity and leadership. Many thinkers believe we are authentic when we act in accordance with our 'inner self' or 'higher self'. This is an essentialist view, believing we have a core essence and if we find and follow this true self, we will be good leaders for business and the community. This is often aligned with religious beliefs. Bill George, one of the major proponents of authenticity, talks of your inner 'True North' and states: 'Your True North begins with the gifts you were given at birth by your Creator' (2007). As coaches and leaders, we can question whether we do actually have an 'inner self' and, if we do, whether it is inherently good.

A different approach to authenticity and authentic leadership comes from Rob Goffee and Gareth Jones, in a series of books and articles from 2000 to the present. For them, authenticity is not innate or essential; it is something that is attributed to you by someone else: 'No leader can look into a mirror and say, "I am authentic." A person cannot be authentic on his or her own' (Goffee and Jones, 2005). They see authenticity as something to be managed, a balance between being true to ourselves and adapting to context. To be effective, we need to adapt to those around us.

In coaching, we find it helpful to use another dimension here (Figure 7.2). We come across some people who are completely themselves, fully authentic with no regard to the impact they have on others. They may be disorganised, overbearing, cruel or lovable, but everyone knows exactly who they are. At the other end of the spectrum are people who are totally focused on how they are perceived by others and who work very hard to manage those perceptions. The common reaction to people like that is, 'I don't know who they are' or 'I don't trust them'.

In coaching, we often use archetypes or real examples from people we know. The over-authentic person might be an 'absent-minded professor' – disorganised, difficult to work with, but admirably completely themselves.

Figure 7.2 The authenticity continuum.

Over-authentic ——————————————————— Over-managed

The over-managed person can be a 'slick politician' whom we think will say anything to win support. If we ask 'who would you like to be led by?', the answer is usually 'neither'. Effective leaders need to be somewhere in the middle. They demonstrate managed authenticity, true enough to themselves that we see them as authentic, but also adapting to context enough to win support and get things done.

This authenticity continuum is usually closely aligned to the organisational savvy continuum we discussed in Chapter 2 on political astuteness. Rather than seeing 'managed authenticity' as a paradox, we see it as a complex balance to be made and remade over time. This helps us deal with the problem of people being 'authentically bad'. We have worked with executives who excuse their bad behaviour as being an expression of their authentic selves. As Donna Ladkin and Chellie Spiller ask, 'When does acting authentically become plain old obstinacy?' (2013). They suggest the notion of a 'self in progress' that allows us to develop over time and to be 'true to oneself' while being open to the truth of another. The self we are committed to is a self in constant development rather than a once- and-for-all project. These ideas of a self in progress and managed authenticity seem to have the most explanatory value and have been of great help in our coaching assignments.

A macro-review of the academic literature by Zhang et al. (2019) identifies the connection between authenticity and positive psychological adjustment generally. Their review also found multiple sources of support for self-compassion as a factor that promotes authenticity, by reducing fear of negative evaluation and raising the level of optimism. Significantly, self-esteem does not appear to be a major factor that influences the level of authenticity.

Being authentic (or being seen as authentic) also increases the amount of collaboration we receive from colleagues (Tang et al., 2021). However, the more organisational politics that are perceived in the system, the less this connection is exhibited.

What we know about networks and networking

Research into social networking suggests that people can on average manage a maximum of 150 strong connections and a much larger number of weak connections (Dunbar, 2010). Strong connections tend to be characterised by a higher quality and frequency of communication, greater trust, greater sense of shared purpose in one or more areas, and more likelihood of putting oneself out for the benefit of the other party. This applies both to individuals and to organisations – studies of company networks show that geographical separation is not a major impediment to the creation and nurturing of informal networks (Casper and Murray, 2002). Weak connections turn out to be more important than might be obvious, especially when it comes to finding new jobs (Granovetter, 1983).

Our strong connections tend to be with people whom we know well and are more likely to be similar to us and have access to similar resources. Our weak connections, with those we are more distant from, can connect us into different networks from our own and bring us a greater diversity of learning and experience.

Having some strong connections to a group of people we fully trust and are close to, combined with a much larger and wider network of weak connections can bring us the most benefit. Robert Putnam (2000) talks about this in terms of balancing our 'bonding capital' with strong connections and our 'bridging capital' which connects us to people different from ourselves.

A research project published in 2016 by Burt and Merluzzi echoes Putnam, finding that the most successful networkers demonstrate 'network oscillation' – switching between deep engagement with a relatively small group and a period of connecting across groups. People who engaged in network oscillation achieved the best results and increased their reputations.

In the context of career development and succession planning, there is potential in being more proactive at both individual and organisational levels. Employees may use their strong connections in other firms either to identify career opportunities directly, or to gain access to these people's own strong or weak connections. When they maintain strong connections within organisations they have left, they may be re-recruited, having gained valuable additional experience and expertise. In industries where employees tend to move between firms relatively quickly (for example, merchant banking or management consultancy), companies save millions of dollars annually because ex-employees turn to their former bosses or mentors for advice when they are ready for their next move. Although there is little empirical evidence to support the proposition, anecdotal evidence suggests that people who devote time and energy to building career-oriented social networks experience faster career progress.

Social networking provides opportunities to engage with a much larger number of weak connections than ever before. And if each of your strong connections is prepared to contact their strong and weak connections on your behalf, the size of your secondary network can potentially be tens of thousands.

There seem to be five main reasons why people build social networks around their job and career needs:

1 *Task information*: what you need to know to be effective in your current roles.
2 *Task achievement*: support in doing your current roles.
3 *Career*: linking with people who can play an active role in furthering your career objectives.
4 *Development*: meeting people who can help with your personal growth and learning.
5 *Mutual support/kinship*: the comfort and confidence that come from knowing that there are other people who share the same issues and concerns as you do, and who can offer mutual help and learning

Research suggests that social networking builds self-esteem (Ellison et al., 2007), probably because it generates a sense of being supported, even though most of the connections may be weak links.

In general, most social networking is unfocused, both in terms of what people give to their networks and the rewards they look to from them. Culture has a role here, with some cultures regarding overt self-promotion as acceptable and others seeing it as gauche and distasteful. At least three of Hofstede's six dimensions of national culture (Hofstede et al., 1990; Gong et al., 2014) have been shown to differ in the context of social media networking. David was reminded of this gulf years ago when a US-based multinational asked him to mediate a dispute between human resources at headquarters and in the UK/Northern Europe over how to interpret employee opinion survey scores. The survey was full of language that had different cultural significance from one side of the Atlantic to the other. For example, in response to the question, 'Do you feel challenged by your work?', the expected response from North America was 'You bet!' In Europe, however, a more typical response was, 'No, I'm coping perfectly well.'

In her book, *Resilience*, Carole Pemberton describes some ad hoc research she carried out into women's attitudes towards networking. She concluded that North American women 'were comfortable with a transactional model based on both parties assessing their mutual career value and then deciding whether to make contact'. Mediterranean women, by contrast, 'operated a relational model, where enjoyment of social contact was the test as to whether any business contact would follow' (2015: 137).

A practical and ethical dilemma for coaches and their clients is, therefore, how do you pitch your communications to cater for such radical differences in expectation and interpretation? Trying to sit in the middle can easily look inauthentic to everyone! One pragmatic solution for coaches and other professionals is to remain within your ethical comfort zone for communications that come directly from you, but to partner with colleagues from other cultures, who are able to present you to their contacts in a more culturally appropriate way. Whichever route you choose, it helps to keep in mind the principles of authentic networking.

Authentic networking

There are four fundamental principles of authentic networking:

1 *Social exchange*: being generous to one's network generates generosity by others.
2 *Clarity*: making your agenda and aspirations transparent.
3 *Awareness*: sensitivity to what is happening in one's network.
4 *Influence*: helping our networks (and others, to which they are connected) find and follow purpose.

Before we examine these, however, it is useful to draw attention to research by Sheena Iyengar and her collaborators, which explores the relationship between being authentic and trying to present your best self when networking.

Irrespective of whether this is at face-to-face social events or online, being yourself results in higher levels of life satisfaction (Bailey et al., 2020). In one of their experiments, peers and speech coaches were asked to rate the effectiveness of corporate executives giving leadership speeches. One group of speakers was asked to reflect upon their core values before their speech, while the others were given no instructions. The former were evaluated much more highly. Iyengar concludes that reconnecting with who we are is a key skill in any important social interaction. She also draws a distinction between networking as a character trait and networking as a skill that can be learned. For coaches and mentors, an implication is that we can help reluctant networkers to both appreciate the difference and reflect upon how to develop greater skills.

Social exchange

Why, when we get an unsolicited sales call, do we typically react so negatively? One reason is that we have no existing social connection, so the call is an intrusion on our privacy. If the caller says that he or she was recommended to speak to you by someone, who is in your social networks, we tend to respond more generously. The second reason is that there is no sense of exchange: 'You don't know me but I'm going to ask you to do me a favour while pretending that I'm doing a favour for you.'

The concept of social exchange is closely allied to that of the psychological contract. A useful model from David's researches into organisational communications identifies three meanings of the word 'value', each attached to a different exchange:

- The Worth exchange is about perceived fairness. In an employer-employee relationship, the employee helps the company create value for customers and in return acquires value in terms of salary, pension and training/experience that makes him or her worth more on the employment market. The cold caller has no psychological contract with me, so I am unlikely to rate the Worth exchange highly.
- The Respect exchange is about the quality of the relationship – do we value each other? Can we learn from each other? Do we show each other courtesy? Do we value the diversity of perspective we offer each other?
- The Meaning or Beliefs exchange is about having shared values. Do we have shared beliefs about ethics, climate change, the role of a coach, and so on? It's not necessary that we share all our core beliefs – just that we share enough to feel a robust connection.

Social exchange is therefore an exchange of value(s) in all senses of the term. The nature of the exchange may be different for different parts of our network – for example, for close personal friends, professional friends and for people who form part of both groups.

In thinking about your *Worth* exchange, consider:

- What do you have to offer in terms of, for example, common cause, information, access to people and other resources?
- What can you gift others in terms of practical support or guidance?
- What are you looking for from others?
- How can you make this as near an equal exchange as possible?
- What can you do to build a deposit of Worth?

A simple example of the last question is a new coach wanting to connect and learn from older hands. She took it upon herself to conduct a review and critique of the literature around a specific area of coaching practice. She then asked the experienced coaches she identified if they would like to have a copy of her paper. Connections made!

In thinking about your *Respect* exchange, consider:

- How can you demonstrate genuine interest and curiosity in the people you want to connect with?
- How would you like them to show respect to you?
- How can you show them appreciation? (For example, by commenting on and adding to their social media posts.)
- How can you show them respectful challenge?
- How can you show that you value the different perspective they bring, while maintaining your own, unique perspective?

In thinking about the *Meaning* or *Beliefs* exchange, consider:

- How clearly do your values come through in your social media posts?
- When is it appropriate for you to seek to connect with someone, on the basis of a shared strong value?
- What impact would it have on you, if someone thanked you for clarifying a value you share? How do you think it would land the other way round?
- How can you engage with a wider network by sharing your reflections on experiences, where your values have been challenged?

Clarity

Clarity relates to both yourself and the purpose of your network. Some pragmatic questions here include:

- Who am I (becoming)?
- What do I want to achieve for myself through networking?
- What do I want to achieve for others or for a greater cause?
- How do those relate to each other? (Are they congruent or divergent?)

- What's the difference you want to make?
- How will you create value for your networks?

One useful metaphor is to think of yourself as a start-up venture. You are making an investment in yourself. What would make other people invest in helping you build your networks? One of the great engines of both commerce and networking is that people who have had successful careers are motivated to support people at the beginning of a similar journey. A key factor is the clarity and scope of the aspirations the younger person expresses. So, have faith in your potential to bring about change and the people, whose support you need, will be attracted towards you.

Awareness

Few, if any, people have just one network. We have multiple, often overlapping networks.

Ibarra and Hunter (2007) describe three types of networking that we engage in. Operational networking, to get work done efficiently, personal networking to enhance our personal and professional development, and strategic networking to figure out future priorities and win stakeholder support for them. Operational networking often involves deep connections for strong working relationships; personal networking is more about breadth, building diverse contacts; while strategic networking tends to focus on leverage, bringing the power to achieve individual and organisational goals.

It's helpful in coaching to think about all three types of networks as many people only focus on one or two of these. As people's careers develop, the importance of strategic networking often increases.

An alternative classification is to think in terms of

- information networks,
- influence networks, and
- support networks.

And how we are active in and need to make use of all three types of network. Awareness is about:

- being clear about the nature of your diverse networks and how they connect to each other (or not)
- being sensitive to what is happening in each network and the implications both for you and for where they overlap.

Useful questions to consider here are:

- What's the nature of your exchange with each of them? (What's the currency in this network?)
- What value am I currently creating in this network?

- What is happening/changing in each of these networks?
- What are the biggest challenges and opportunities for each of these networks?
- What are the implications for you in those challenges and opportunities?
- What emerging themes are common to several of your networks?
- What does each network NOT want from me?
- What are the implications of being in network A for what I can achieve with network B?

An example of the latter is a network of 'global gurus', in which David is regularly featured. The organisers encourage those people on the list to reach out to their followers to vote for their ranking. He is also engaged with several networks promoting ethicality in coaching. The two networks have drastically opposing values. No prizes for guessing which he chooses to be active in!

By being clear about how we select who we network with and why, we can be much more selective and purposeful about network-building. With practice, most people can become quite skilled at evaluating potential new connections against the social exchange criteria above.

Clarity also helps us distinguish between quantity and quality. Before reaching out to connect with someone you don't know, consider:

- How will this connection add value for both of us?
- How will they fit into or augment my existing networks?

A key aspect of quality is the super-connector – the influencer, who is connected to substantial numbers of other influencers. The distinction between quality and quantity is critical here. Someone with 100,000 or more followers isn't going to have personal time to even know you exist! Some considerations in deciding whether someone is a genuine super-connector are as follows:

- Are their posts and website driven by self-promotion or cause-driven?
- Do they respond personally to contacts? (How they find the time is a mystery, but super-connectors typically respond to every genuine request!)
- How peer-oriented are they? (Have they a track record of growing peers?)

Super-connectors are most likely to respond when they conclude that:

- you have read their work
- you are genuinely curious
- you have some original thoughts, insights or experience to share through the super-connector to others in their network.

When thinking about quality versus quantity, it's important we don't go too far in the direction of quality. We know from the concept of weak ties that there is a benefit in large, diverse networks. We have worked with executives who have been too focused on the quality of their networking, trying to connect to the perfect person in the perfect way. Rather than spending this energy on one connection, it is often more beneficial to build ten weaker connections. Some of these may develop into strong connections over time. In terms of influence, or being considered for an opportunity, the wider your network, the better. Often decisions are made in rooms that we aren't invited to. We need someone in the room to mention us when a potential opportunity or need is discussed. That person doesn't necessarily have to be very strongly aligned with us, but they have to be in the right place at the right time. The more people who know about us, the more likely one of our connections is going to be in that room.

Influence

Influence is about connecting others so they can:

* achieve more together than they can apart
* find common purpose
* achieve collective voice.

Some questions for consideration here include:

* What are legitimate purposes for parts or all of your network?
* How can I help parts of my network create more purposeful and influential connections?
* How can I help those in my networks achieve influence for good?
* What collaborations can I stimulate? (Whether or not I become one of the collaborators.)
* What other networks could we influence together and how?

The roles of coaches, mentors and sponsors

One way of understanding the roles of coaches, mentors and sponsors is that:

* coaches help you develop your reputation and political management skills in general
* mentors help you navigate the political environment in a particular context – for example, an organisation or profession
* sponsors open the doors to progression for you and may manage the politics on your behalf, or give help on specific issues.

While this is a simplistic perspective, it has value in defining broadly what kind of support to seek and when. Problems arise when coaching or mentoring become entangled with sponsorship. This happens much more frequently in the US than Europe, because organisations in Europe believe that sponsorship is incompatible with mentoring or coaching when both roles are taken by the same person (Bhide and Tootell, 2018). In particular, sponsorship involves a different power dimension. It is about the exercise of political power, rather than supporting someone in navigating the political system.

Authentic sponsorship is an under-researched topic. Issues to consider as a sponsor include:

- Whose agenda is the sponsorship relationship following? Your own? That of the organisation's? The sponsee's?
- How open is the agenda?
- How will you manage the confidentiality issues? (Usually very clear in coaching and mentoring, they can be much muddier in sponsorship.)
- What reciprocity is involved? (Sponsors often expect loyalty in return. Is this appropriate?)
- How will you encourage openness in the relationship, when the sponsee will typically want you to think the best of them and be reluctant to expose their weaknesses to you?
- Should you support the promotion of fatally flawed individuals?

For the coach or mentor, issues to consider with regard to networking include:

- To what extent should you open your networks to the client?
- What criteria will you use in deciding when and how?
- How will you help them develop the social connections and networks they need to be successful?

A good starting point is this five-stage process:

Stage 1: Encourage the client to map out their existing networks, on a large sheet of paper or using a computer program. How do each of the people in these networks support them in achieving their long-term, medium-term and short-term objectives – directly and indirectly? It can be helpful to rate these connections in different ways, depending on the context. For example:

- How well do you know that person? How well do they know you?
- How much do you trust that person? How much do they trust you?
- How much do you like that person? How much do they like you?
- How much influence can that person have over what you want to achieve?
- How can you help them achieve their goals?

Reviewing your network in this way can help you spot strengths and also weaknesses and gaps that you want to work on and also identify areas where you need to learn more.

Stage 2: Help them to design their *ideal* social network. Who would appear in it and what function would they play?

Stage 3: Who could provide the links between their existing networks and the ideal?

Stage 4: What will they offer to each stage of these networks to make others want to be in their network?

Stage 5: What can they do right now, drawing on their strengths and interests, to start to construct their ideal network?

An important conversation revolves around balancing the creation of more effective social exchange with their existing networks and creating new connections. There are no hard and fast rules here, but a suggested guideline is to put as much effort and attention into strengthening existing connections as developing new weak ones.

More generally, with regard to reputation management, the following questions can be powerful in helping the client focus on what is important:

- What kind of reputation is valuable in terms of advancement in this organisation?
- Who has an influence on your reputation? (This may include boss, colleagues, direct reports and customers.)
- How do these people perceive you? How can you find out? How can you obtain honest, accurate and timely feedback on how others perceive you?
- How has your reputation affected your career so far?
- What do you want to be recognised for?
- How will this help you achieve your performance and/or career goals?
- How does this relate to your ideal self?
- What changes do you need to make, to build a reputation that is positive and justified?
- Who can help you do this?

Another way for coaches and mentors to support their clients on networking is to think in terms of information, influence and support networks. These questions are helpful here – and of course leaders can also ask them of themselves! You can begin by asking who is in each of these networks now and then looking at how to develop them further.

Questions to ask when building information networks:

- Where is the important information you need?
- How can you design and develop a network to access this information?
- Which key groups and individuals will have critical interests related to your work?

- How can you devise a network that will help you understand the interests of involved groups and estimate their relative power?
- How can you use your network to monitor attitudes and reactions over time?

Questions to ask when building influence networks:

- What influence do you need?
- Who are the key people who have influence?
- What makes them influential in the system?
- How can you mobilise their energy to help you neutralise their potential opposition or overcome their apathy/resistance?
- How can you influence key external stakeholders to promote and support you?
- If you cannot influence them directly, who do you know who can?

Questions to ask when building support networks:

- Who in the system is prepared to support you?
- Are there people with whom you can discuss your role?
- Do you have objective and informed listeners to keep you and your reactions in perspective?
- Who can provide you with emotional support when things get tough?
- When do you use your support network?
- How could you improve it?

A final exercise that we find useful with people we are working with on networking is to look in terms of the past, present and future. This can prompt people to take appropriate actions now.

- *Past*: Who used to be in your network, but you have lost contact with?
- *Present*: Who is in your network, but you should strengthen the relationship?
- *Future*: Who is not in your network, who you would like to build a relationship with?

How to be a good networker

In the light of all of the above and our belief in the need for high-integrity political engagement, what other advice is there to be a good networker?

Ibarra and Hunter recommend that we give and take continually. They advise that we don't just take and don't just network when we need something. This clearly aligns with Adam Grant's (2021) recommendation to be a Smart Giver, discussed further in Chapter 2. In his book *Never Eat Alone* (2005),

Keith Ferrazzi includes practical advice on networking, including to be genuine and 'don't be a networking jerk' by only looking at what you can gain.

Based on the insights of these experts, here is some high-integrity networking advice that we share with people we work with:

- Establish diverse connections, create reasons to interact outside your own area.
- Make it a habit to purposefully connect with people often. Be proactive and assertive, take the initiative.
- Give and take continually. Don't just take and don't just network when you need something.
- Build your network before you need it.
- Be honest, transparent and trustworthy.
- Truly connect with people, think in the long term.
- Build intimacy quickly, talk about important things.
- Share your passions, combine them with networking.
- Develop conversational currency, have something to say.
- Be interesting, share your opinions and views.
- Let others know who you are.
- Be a better listener, listen more than you talk.
- Be clear, ask for what you want. Don't expect people to read your mind. Ask for and offer help.
- Say thank you, acknowledge favours and help.
- Follow up and keep your word.
- Don't keep score, don't be too efficient.
- Don't take yourself too seriously.
- Be courageous, feel the fear and do it anyway.

Conclusion

We believe that we can and should positively engage with organisational power and politics at work. An important part of doing that is to build and use effective networks and consciously develop our social presence. In today's complex, changing and interconnected world, it's very rare for an individual to be able to achieve what they want alone. A lot of our strength lies in our ability to engage with and work with different people and that relies on our networking abilities.

Again, it's largely about balance. Not being only self- or other-focused. Not being only authentic or over-managed but finding and maintaining a balance of managed authenticity.

Being clear about what you want from networking, building real connections and helping others will enable you to build the networks you need for success. Balancing time in close-knit bonding networks, with time in more diverse bridging networks, is likely to be most effective. We need to be our authentic, distinct selves and to develop and apply networking skills. Goffee and Jones's (2000) work on leadership and authenticity is helpful here and we'll conclude with their advice: 'Be yourself – more – with skill.'

References

Bailey, E.R., Matz, S.C., Youyou, W. and Iyengar, S.S. (2020) Authentic self-expression on social media is associated with greater subjective well-being, *Nature Communications*, 11 (1): 1–9.

Bhide, V. and Tootell, B. (2018) Perceptions of sponsoring as a career advancement tool for women: Are they different in Europe?, *International Journal of Evidence Based Coaching and Mentoring*, 16 (1): 3–19.

Burt, R. and Merluzzi, J. (2016) Network oscillation, *Academy of Management Discoveries*, 2 (4): 368–391.

Casper, S. and Murray, F. (2002) Careers and clusters: Analyzing the career network dynamic of biotechnology clusters, *Journal of Engineering and Technology Management*, 22 (1/2): 51–74.

Clutterbuck, D. and Dearlove, D. (1995) *Routes to the Top*. London: Kinsley Lord.

Dunbar, R. (2010) *How Many Friends Does One Person Need?* London: Faber & Faber.

Ellison, N.B., Steinfeld, C. and Lampe, C. (2007) The benefits of Facebook 'friends': Social capital and college students' use of online social network sites, *Journal of Computer-Mediated Communication*, 12 (4): 1143–1168.

Ferrazzi, K. (2005) *Never Eat Alone*. New York: Doubleday.

George, B. (2007) *The spirituality of authentic leadership*. Available at: https://www.billgeorge.org/articles/the-spirituality-of-authentic-leadership/.

Goffee, R. and Jones, G. (2000) Why should anyone be led by you?, *Harvard Business Review*, September/October. Available at: https://hbr.org/2000/09/why-should-anyone-be-led-by-you.

Goffee, R. and Jones, G. (2005) Managing authenticity: The paradox of great leadership, *Harvard Business Review*, December. Available at: https://hbr.org/2005/12/managing-authenticity-the-paradox-of-great-leadership.

Gong, W., Stump, R.L. and Li, Z.G. (2014) Global use and access of social networking web sites: A national culture perspective, *Journal of Research in Interactive Marketing*, 8: 183–188.

Granovetter, M. (1983) The strength of weak ties: A network theory revisited, *Sociological Theory*, 1: 201–233.

Grant, A (2021) *Think Again*. London: Penguin Random House.

Hofstede, G., Neuijen, B., Ohayv, D.D. and Sanders, G. (1990) Measuring organizational cultures: A qualitative and quantitative study across twenty cases, *Administrative Science Quarterly*, 35 (2): 286–316.

Ibarra, H. and Hunter, M. (2007) How leaders create and use networks, *Harvard Business Review*, January. Available at: https://hbr.org/2007/01/how-leaders-create-and-use-networks.

Ladkin, D. and Spiller, C. (2013) When does acting authentically become plain old obstinacy?, Elgar [blog]. Available at: https://elgar.blog/2013/10/31/when-does-acting-authentically-become-plain-old-obstinacy-by-donna-ladkin-and-chellie-spiller/ [accessed January 2022].

Mengers, A. (2014) *The benefits of being yourself: An examination of authenticity, uniqueness, and well-being*, Master of Applied Positive Psychology (MAPP) thesis, University of Pennsylvania, Capstone Projects 63. Available at: https://repository. upenn.edu/mapp_capstone/63.

Pemberton, C. (2015) *Resilience: A practical guide for coaches*. Maidenhead: Open University Press.

Putnam, R.D. (2000) *Bowling Alone: The collapse and revival of American community*. New York: Simon & Schuster.

Sedikides, C., Meek, R., Alicke, M.D. and Taylor, S. (2014) Behind bars but above the bar: Prisoners consider themselves more prosocial than non-prisoners, *British Journal of Social Psychology*, 53 (2): 396–403.

Tang, Y.P., Xu, E., Huang, X. and Pu, X. (2021) When can display of authenticity at work facilitate coworker interactions? The moderating effect of perception of organizational politics, *Human Relations*, 76 (1). Available at: https://doi.org/10.1177 %2F00187267211031834.

Toor, S.R. and Ofori, G. (2009) Authenticity and its influence on psychological well-being and contingent self-esteem of leaders in Singapore construction sector, *Construction Management and Economics*, 27 (3): 299–313.

Zhang, J.W., Chen, S., Tomova Shakur, T.K., Bilgin, B., Chai, W.J., Ramis, T., Shaban-Azad, H., Razavi, P., Nutankumar, T. and Manukyan, A. (2019) A compassionate self is a true self? Self-compassion promotes subjective authenticity, *Personality and Social Psychology Bulletin*, 45 (9): 1323–1337.

8 The politics of a digital world

Tim Bright and David Clutterbuck

The world that organisations operate in is becoming more digital. The Covid-19 pandemic dramatically accelerated a shift to digital, remote and flexible working. Some companies are aiming to move back to their previous way of working with everyone in the workplace all the time, but a lot of companies are embracing flexible, hybrid and digital working to a greater or lesser degree. We are all relying more on technology and communicating more and more through technological methods and less in person.

How does organisational politics function in this new world? What is good practice for informal power relationships in the digital world? And how can coaches support their clients effectively?

One perspective on politics is that of change versus stability. In a VUCA world, this dynamic is emphasised. In particular, new technologies bring disruption to hierarchies, boundaries and ways of working. These disruptions are often analysed in the contexts of resilience, resistance to change and psychological safety – but rarely, if ever, as an issue of politics. Taking a political perspective means asking questions, such as:

- Who stands to gain and lose from this change? And how?
- What are the personal and group risks from engaging with the change?
- What are the personal and group risks from ignoring it?

Uncertainty also plays a role. Resistance to change increases if people cannot predict whether the outcome will enhance or diminish their status, their autonomy, their security, and so on. If they feel that any of these are already under threat, their overall level of anxiety will be amplified.

Organisational politics in the digital world will impact us in different areas.

Digital working

The Covid-19 pandemic sped up the move towards virtual team meetings and working from home, which in turn induced subtle changes in team dynamics. Team leaders' control had to be relaxed (although some companies reinforced it by measuring the number of keystrokes employees performed every hour!), giving team members greater autonomy. In teams, where some members were previously co-located with the leader and others distributed, a subtle shift in power occurred. When everyone is virtual, they are more equal in terms of access to the key conversations that shape policy. Many of our clients have reported that moving to virtual work has made things more democratic. Everyone is the same size on the screen in a Zoom call.

One of Tim's clients with a large concentration of staff in one head office location, plus smaller teams throughout the world, noticed a significant shift of power during the pandemic. Previously, people in the overseas offices felt at a disadvantage, connecting to meetings remotely while the head office team sat together in a meeting room. That changed during the pandemic. Because everyone was connecting to meetings remotely, those from around the world no longer felt disadvantaged compared with the people in head office and they experienced that their voices were heard more and they could have more impact on decisions. This organisation has decided to keep some meetings online permanently for all participants for this reason, and all will connect via their individual screens even if they are in the same location.

Also, in our experience we have seen teams working together remotely being more disciplined and observing better practices in meetings in terms of listening, not interrupting and taking turns. This has allowed a better quality of interaction to take place, engaging a wider variety of participants.

Use of different technological tools has also encouraged engagement. In meetings we have facilitated, some who may not feel comfortable speaking up have used the text chat function to get their points across and this has given them more of a voice. Also, use of text in meetings has enabled a different quality of thinking and participation. As facilitators, we have asked participants to write their thoughts on a particular issue and then to all share that text at once, using the chat function. This engages everyone in reflective thinking time and also means that everybody's thoughts are noticed, rather than only the most high-status or extrovert participants. Use of online polls is also a simple way to increase engagement. These tools or similar can be used in physical meetings but they are more likely to be used in online settings.

If organisations return to more in-person meetings, then these remote workers stand to lose the status and influence they have gained. Currently, we and others are noticing that remote meetings work well, as do in-person meetings. The least effective meetings seem to be when some participants are gathered in a room together and others connect remotely. Inevitably, there is more nuanced and effective communication between those sitting physically together, and those dialling in experience less power. Good practice seems to be to get everyone to connect through their own screens, even if some of them are in the same building, so that all have the same meeting experience.

The direct close-up contact of video calls can also lead to a greater sense of immediacy and attention. Also, we have seen into each other's home lives as we have become more relaxed and comfortable with these tools. A number of our clients have expressed how physical remoteness has been combined with a stronger sense of connection. In a number of our clients we have seen that employee engagement scores rose during the pandemic. This seems to be due to the increased flexibility that employees have enjoyed, and also due to a greater sense of purpose that some felt working during the pandemic.

The timing of international virtual meetings also has a political dimension in that it creates a ranking order about whose time and wellbeing are most important. Who is expected to attend at unsocial hours? How equally is the pain distributed? Is it even discussed? An international team that Tim has worked with spent time to carefully plot all the team members' time zones onto a PowerPoint slide and agree which hours were appropriate for meetings.

Work from anywhere

As more companies have moved to fully remote working, working from home has also developed into working from anywhere. A number of companies were using this approach for years before the pandemic, allowing employees to work from anywhere around the world, in any time zone. To manage asynchronous working, these companies have developed new ways of working that involve a lot of transparency and recording many issues in writing, so everyone has access to them. Github has been a pioneer in this area and has shared their own Remote Playbook online (https://about.gitlab.com/company/culture/all-remote/).

Github's Remote Manifesto includes principles such as:

- Writing down and recording knowledge over verbal explanations.
- Written-down processes over on-the-job training.
- Public sharing of information over need-to-know access.
- Opening up every document for editing by anyone over top-down control of documents.
- Asynchronous communication over synchronous communication.
- Formal communication channels over informal communication channels.

It remains to be seen how these approaches will impact organisational politics, but it seems reasonable to assume that asynchronous working, with more decisions and processes being shared in writing, will create a more level playing field for employees and could encourage greater inclusion. Github's preference for formal over informal communication channels may also encourage greater equality across the organisation as it removes some of the implicit power and access differences in informal communication.

It's also noteworthy that companies working in this way have a tendency towards greater transparency. Buffer is another company which has been fully remote since 2015 and shares its learnings openly online (https://buffer.com/resources/remote-work/). Buffer also is completely transparent about salaries in the company and shares the amounts paid and methods of calculation online (https://buffer.com/salaries). This transparency is likely to improve the conditions of disadvantaged groups over time.

Digital reputations

Digital social media transcend organisational boundaries and can make or break reputations. The power of connection has always been a political game-changer but the rules of connection have now changed. Whether at work or in wider society, digital technology has enabled the rise of the influencer, who creates their influence through their skills of connecting. Boundaries between 'in-groups' and 'out-groups are far more fluid than they have historically been.

Negative politics isn't going away

Our increasingly digital world is not all positive for organisational politics.

The idea of being in an inner or outer circle as discussed in Chapter 6 on gender can become even more important. You might have no idea that some meetings are happening without you, or that certain networks exist, because they are all going on virtually between people working remotely. There is a risk that remote working solidifies divides that already exist and makes it harder for people to challenge existing power relationships.

Physical interactions are likely to become more important. When the 'Big Bang' liberalised financial markets in the UK in the late 1980s and allowed much more use of technology, there was an expectation that property prices in the City of London would drop as location became less important. In fact, the reverse happened. When information is spread more widely and instantly, the few rare titbits that you can pick up in person become even more valuable, so physically being near other players became even more important. In hybrid working we may well see the same kind of trend. Who can afford to continue to live in expensive central locations and come more often physically together, and will they get privileged access to power compared to people working remotely in cheaper locations? Will companies pay to bring all their remote employees together for specific meetings, or only a selected group, and how will that affect power dynamics?

We have talked above about the importance of presence in online meetings. Power and privilege will continue to have an impact. Who is able to use an HD webcam and have good lighting, a fast internet connection and a quiet uninterrupted environment to work in at home, to be able to focus on their work and make a good impression when meeting online?

As different forms of virtual and augmented reality become more common, how you present yourself in this environment is significant. Are you given or do you buy an impressive avatar? Will virtual avatars or metaverse clothing purchases become the new version of 'power dressing'?

Existing power structures don't disappear in the digital world and may become even more intensely differentiated.

Coaching in the digital world

All of this is significant for coaches on a number of dimensions. First, it's easier to break into coaching markets. The power of connection and skill at marketing assume greater import vis-à-vis competence, skill and experience, than would have been the case just a few years ago. Second, coaches need to be digitally skilled, in order to operate within and recognise the challenges their clients face in digital politics. Coaches also need to have stronger skills of systemic awareness, to understand how politics are expressed in an ever-more-connected environment (Bürgi et al., 2023).

Artificial Intelligence (AI) is rapidly becoming a third party in coaching relationships. Most of what is currently available is in the form of coachbots – routine algorithms that manage a structured coaching process, such as GROW. However, the next generations of AI have much greater autonomy on the questions they ask and the information they gather – for example, through observing body language or voice tone. Much of this data will not be observable by the human coach. There is increasing concern about how much power and control the AI will take from the coach as it gradually increases in capability. One of the interesting aspects of this evolution is that the AI has no *political intent*.

It's up to us

All technical developments in history have the potential to be used for positive or destructive purposes. For coaches, and everyone who works in organisations, it is up to us to understand the implications of new ways of working and intentionally use them to increase diversity, equity, inclusion and belonging. The fundamentals of informal power and political relationships haven't changed. Political astuteness can still be used for good or bad aims. The changes of the digital world offer great opportunities for democratisation and breaking down boundaries, but we must work intentionally to ensure these potential gains are really achieved and not just replaced by different forms of privilege. We all need to hone our political astuteness for the developing digital world and ensure that we work in the most effective ways to reach our organisational goals with integrity.

Reference

Bürgi, M., Ashok, M. and Clutterbuck, D. (2023) Ethics and the digital environment in coaching, in W.A. Smith, J. Passmore, E. Turner, Y.L. Lai and D. Clutterbuck (eds) *The Ethical Coaches' Handbook: A Guide to Developing Ethical Maturity in Practice*. London: Routledge.

Leadership for tomorrow

Lise Lewis

Introduction

'I can't be bothered with office politics – it's a waste of time and a distraction – I find I get irritated with those who aren't committed', stated a future client of my coaching practice. The coaching brief was to improve team relationships for this senior leader who prefers the technical element of the role. The challenge was bringing together a multinational team – or possibly best described by the future client as a fragmented group comprising at least three different cultures. Hearing the reaction to 'office politics' I revisited the comment by inviting the leader's interpretation of organisational politics, observing whether the reaction possibly contributed to the apparent team dysfunction and encouraging a conversation about the consequences of dismissing politics. The wish not to 'be bothered with office politics' prompts the question: 'How important is being aware of and engaging with organisational politics to the leadership role?'

This chapter examines themes that are currently having an impact on the workplace and have a political dimension as being only a part of the bigger picture of leadership:

- Defining leadership for the future of work
- How leaders describe the political dimension of their roles
- How leaders set the political climate for their organisations
- Macro-politics: leadership challenges when connecting the organisation with the wider system is the primary topic for this chapter
- The impact of global disruption informs how the workplace is likely to evolve, how organisational politics feature and how leadership may have to adapt to the future world of work by adjusting to the:
  - catastrophic effect of the Covid-19 pandemic
  - alarming environmental damage
  - pace of change in technology affecting competitive edge
  - noticeable deterioration of wellbeing in the workforce and what changes can be anticipated that will reconfigure employment contracts
  - evolving shape of leadership emerging from this transforming world of work: social and psychological capability.

Defining leadership for the future of work

To be alert to the impact of global disruption, I see leaders of the future proactively:

- driving Collaboration to enhance productivity
- demonstrating Compassion for self and others in facing unexpected challenges
- being kind and Caring in turbulent times
- Communicating for understanding by speaking with genuine intent and reflection to gain mutual understanding.

Combined with David Clutterbuck's four Cs of leadership – Courage, Curiosity, Connectedness and also Compassion – gives a composite offering of seven Cs.

Consistently demonstrating these attributes is likely beyond the capability of even the most successful leader as leaders are human too and subject to the same influences that affect us all. With the current level of global instability, leaders are facing exceptional demands on their ability to continuously engage with altruistic practices. In these times, how organisational politics feature as enabling and disabling organisational functioning will also necessitate vigorous examination.

How leaders describe the political dimension of their roles

Quotes explicitly or implicitly referencing politics in leadership have appeared since the time of Aristotle, who wrote that 'politics stems from a diversity of interests, and those competing interests must be resolved in some way'. Leaders can use 'positive' political activity to benefit and empower others fairly and appropriately and through awareness of 'negative' politics can avoid disabling behaviours by those wishing to gain advantage.

This sample of quotes from past and current world leaders declares their beliefs that are either created – or likely – to steer the political landscape within their organisations or the causes they champion:

People is the most important thing in an organization – I interpret 'is the most important thing' to describe people as being a comment having positive intent.
– Pablo Isla, until 2022 Chairman and CEO of Inditex,
a large Spanish corporation

Life's too short to hang out with people who aren't resourceful – choosing to focus on those who are productive – the 80% as in the Pareto concept.
– Jeff Bezos, Executive Chairman of Amazon

You should never let your fears prevent you from doing what you know is right – a belief demonstrating courageous leadership for altruistic reasons.
– Aung San Suu Kyi, former State Counsellor of Myanmar, Leader of the National League for Democracy and currently imprisoned

A genuine leader is not a searcher for consensus but a molder of consensus – encouraging collaboration for shared ownership of decisions.
– Martin Luther King, Jr.

Any time you start something new [like an innovation initiative] that cuts across many areas, there's a potential for people feeling like you're in their backyard and is especially true when the core business is successful and doing well – identifying people's propensity for competition when vying for recognition of personal achievements.
– Michael Britt, President and CEO Southern Telecom

Determination, energy, and courage appear spontaneously when we care deeply about something. We take risks that are unimaginable in any other context – highly motivated to succeed against all odds for an outcome or cause that meets personal values and inner satisfaction.
– Margaret J. Wheatley, Management Consultant and Writer

Although I offer an interpretation of these quotes, only the owners know their true and intentioned meaning. When compared with the attributes defining leadership at the start of this chapter, we can notice how such quotes can be interpreted in determining the political direction of the organisation.

The people perspective is already well-used when recognising that 'organisations are people' and how the political climate is perceived determines consequent behaviour. How well do people feel cared for, does the quality of communication facilitate understanding, and does leadership effectively find avenues for collaboration? Leaders know it's impossible to resolve every political disagreement, often based on perceived inequalities such as unequal sharing of resources. However, the politically aware leader avoids entanglement in such scenarios by remedying unfair practices – when these exist – and in all situations being clear about what everyone's contribution is expected to be.

Staying alert and noticing early signs of changes in the market informs the speedy redefinition of business strategy. Establishing an informed redesign of the working environment, acknowledging positive behaviours, rewarding diverse viewpoints and recruiting fresh talent encourage a sense of belonging and connectedness between employees when feeling part of an innovative team facing current challenges.

The intention here is to reinforce the function of organisational politics as making a positive contribution to healthy organisations without denying that undermining influences exist when humans bring alternative personal agendas to the workplace. Enlightened leaders tend to avoid political destabilisation by communicating strong messages reinforcing a culture of the way things 'are done around here'.

Systemic influences cannot be ignored. The current war in Ukraine and the restrictions on energy by Russia have caused escalating world inflation affecting corporate budgets and the ability of organisations to remain viable. The courageous leader makes what can be unpalatable political decisions when reacting to world events that threaten the viability of commercial activities and stimulates curiosity that leads to creativity in finding solutions during times of recession. Compassionate leadership recognises the tensions and stresses in these unprecedented times and builds capacity for resilience.

How leaders set the political climate for their organisations

What you do has far greater impact than what you say.

– Stephen Covey

Chapter 1 outlined our survey findings and identified leaders as consistently identifying organisational politics as:

- always present and part of the working routine
- a display of power dynamics both covert and overt
- a way to influence outcomes by knowing how and who to talk with to gain a preferred outcome
- a way to advance self-interests under the guise of being helpful
- used in service of self-preservation to maintain a sense of safety.

These responses may endorse a sense of reality that organisational politics being both positive and negative reflects the human condition as having the capability of taking either position; the difference depending on the choices we make in a given context.

Answers to the question 'What is your own view of politics within an organisation?' saw 58% of leaders choose the response 'neither a good or bad thing – it all depends on the motivation and how it is put into practice', with 16% believing that politics are 'a necessary evil' and 25% saying politics are 'to be avoided at all costs'. Only one responder thought that politics are 'by and large positive'. Almost

90% believed that leaders need to have political astuteness. These results appear to suggest having a level of caution when immersed in organisational politics.

A sample of qualitative statements from leaders responding to our survey are selected for further interpretation (see Chapter 1 for a comprehensive analysis of research data):

Positive intentions:

* *manage relationships in a balance to protect interests of all involved as well as protecting own stance*
* *walking the talk – showing clearly that negative political games have no place in the organisation by calling them out and stopping them*
* *affecting real change, sustainable development and growth; developing partnerships and alliances; having a real impact on people's lives*
* *fostering diversity and inclusion – means you can unlock the full potential of the organization*
* *trust between the leaders – again this permeates the rest of the organisation's behaviours together – there are less barriers and we get more done.*

Negative influences:

* *an unnecessary distraction when it's not coming from a place of positive intent*
* *individual positioning often for resources and access to more power to make decisions*
* *power play between individuals and groups*
* *use of power, authority, information to manage the business towards one's agenda*
* *generally ends up being driven away from company results – through distraction.*

I draw on personal experiences of a previously held role as president of a global organisation, functioning on voluntary support, to illustrate briefly the qualitative statements quoted above. As a scene-setter, the organisation is a professional body structured as a federation with several thousand members spread across 26 countries and two regions. Each country affiliated to the organisation creates policy and working practices appropriate to the local membership with strategic direction generated at global level by a council of country presidents, and operationally delivered by an executive board.

Together with executive board colleagues, my intention as president was to take as democratic an approach as possible to encourage fairness and equity in meeting the interests of all stakeholders. The aim was to maintain and sustain a viable organisation through organic growth, matching available volunteer support and to raise the quality of mentoring, coaching and supervision through pioneering professional standards of practice ultimately for the benefit of society. The inherent challenges of operating on an international platform, respecting cultural differences and working with the diverse expectations of volunteers made nurturing productive relationships an essential and regular practice. This meant making time to communicate widely and regularly, listening and being sensitive to local needs within the context of strategic aspirations and possibilities. Clearly, not everything is possible and inevitably people are disappointed. I believed in transparency within a framework of politically viable decision-making. Making everything known all of the time without consideration for consequences is politically naïve. Some situations were best managed at individual level where opposing expectations had the potential for disruption and others were managed more effectively through consultation and collaboration across a wider range of stakeholders.

Political activities were not always easy to notice, given the geography of the organisation and the different aspirations of volunteers both individually and collectively. My approach was to trust that everyone was working towards the common purpose unless actions proved otherwise. Once noticed, opposing divisions were best challenged at source. I remember a particularly difficult situation that threatened to rupture the organisation and realised the only choice for damage limitation was to confront the situation openly at the next full leadership meeting that included the initiators of the disruptive agendas. This was a difficult decision, took courage and kept me awake the night before reflecting on how to reveal an unacceptable situation whilst maintaining cohesion within the leadership.

Naturally, every organisation has 'unnecessary distractions', often generated when individuals have unrealised strong personal agendas. I recall other instances of being in dialogue with colleagues, reflecting and seeking solutions to issues where an individual or group of individuals were keen to follow a course of action that was favourable to them and not to the majority within the organisation. This is inevitable where decisions made in the best interests of the local population disadvantages the wider population. Rationale can be diminished to endorse favourite projects and when dissent is seen as a barrier to fulfilling personal needs. I found these among the most difficult times to choose when to trust and when to be cautious. Consulting dependable colleagues is essential in gaining perspective between what is genuine and what is fabrication of the facts designed to protect personal interests.

Working with a multicultural team was undoubtedly a rich experience when individual passions surfaced to overtly challenge differing beliefs and clashed when igniting conflicting temperaments and personalities. I found a sense of humour was indispensable as a soothing balm for calming 'ruffled feathers'.

Macro-politics: how leadership connects the organisation with its environment

The workplace of tomorrow: What is influencing the Leadership Landscape?

Introducing what seems to be shaping the workplace of tomorrow is the foundation for leading into – later in the chapter – how organisational politics are likely to feature in this new world.

We're familiar with hearing the descriptor 'hybrid' as defining the current and anticipated model of working practices. 'Hybrid' working referring only to flexibility with the place of work seems to have been ejected in favour of 'flexible working' that will be used to cover working hours, the place of work, the time the employee is required to work and much more.

The Covid-19 pandemic

We know the unexpected explosion of Covid-19 around the world has revolutionised the complexion of how we work today and reports indicate this is likely to be semi-permanent and probably permanent in some sectors. Leaders were catapulted into the unknown and generally unprepared for the tensions that the coronavirus presented to working practices.

Fast-forwarding to when hopefully coronavirus will be controlled by mass immunisation, perhaps the most radical change jettisons the traditional routine of daily hours and number of days worked into the redundancy shredder. Flexible working has taken on a whole new meaning. Employees who once appreciated flexible working as a privilege offered by enlightened employers are now interchanging 'flexible' with 'fixed' as expectations for nominating hours of employment become standard practice.

Forced into the 'work at home' consequence of coronavirus opened new horizons for the workplace. Organisations as well as employees had to be agile in responding to this compulsory shift. Stories of balancing laptops on tops of washing machines placed a health burden necessitating ergonomically safer workstations. The withdrawal of the social aspect of work caused some to feel isolated, whilst those with a preference for introversion welcomed the solace of solitude to help concentration. Some thrived and some found the stress of homeworking affected their mental health. Some were reluctant to return to the formality and perceived constraints of 'office working' when enjoying the work/life balance that stemmed and flowed from choosing when to work. The profile of family life integrated rather than competed with the day job.

Living with coronavirus is becoming the norm as more people are vaccinated to protect against or at least reduce the seriousness of becoming infected; coronavirus has been likened to the new 'flu'. Although health issues appear to be taking a downward trajectory, change created by the pandemic continues. 'Working from home is now a permanent fixture, say bosses' was the headline of a *Times* of London report (2022) recording the following statistics:

- >25% of 700 executives surveyed expect to agree to employees choosing their working patterns
- 79% of leaders polled by the Institute of Directors plan to adopt remote working in the long term
- only 16% will 'demand' that staff go into the workplace 5 days a week
- a poll by 'Slack', the workplace collaboration tool, reports that 1 in 6 white-collar workers are prepared to change jobs if forced to return to the office.

Clearly, returning to the 'norm' of business routine appears displaced by the new world of 'work how and when you wish as long as the job gets done'. Few in the UK could have predicted such a seismic shift in work patterns not experienced probably since the Industrial Revolution in the eighteenth century when people moved from the farm to the factory for work. Employees now are likely to become more mobile in employment and be attracted to those organisations with the most favourable benefits, eschewing the demotivating restrictions of returning to 'how things used to be' in the workplace.

Many are likely to miss the 'buzz' of the office and will happily return to the daily commute. What's different is that a taste of choosing when and how you work lingers and return to work doesn't necessarily mean everyone wants to or is even willing to fit back into a 'one option' of work pattern. Flexibility is likely to become the future trend for working practices as employees resist or possibly refuse the fixed working week contract. Clearly, unemployment levels will influence the ability to choose terms and conditions of employment. What is likely is that employment packages will be challenged as individuals in sectors of high employment will make their job selection based on an employment offer of best fit with their work/life preferences. Childcare policies seem an obvious area to review where parents can arrange their working day to meet family needs.

One question is, can companies offer acceptable flexible work policies that entice people back to the workplace and how will leaders cope with distributed team working? If organisational politics are viewed as a 'display of power dynamics' and a way to influence outcomes, we can speculate how this may shift the balance more towards employees when negotiating employment packages.

'The four-day working week is taking off, with 70 UK firms and more than 3,300 employees taking part in a new trial. During the six-month pilot, staff will work a shorter week with no loss of pay', writes Frost (2022). This trial of working practice is designed to assess whether 100% productivity can be achieved 80% of the time. Might we speculate this as a politically perceptive leadership strategy to satisfy employees' wish for shorter hours whilst maintaining the required level of productivity to remain profitable? Might we also see the leadership attributes of exercising 'curiosity' about this creative way of working and demonstrating a 'caring' attitude to a preferred way of working?

Damage to the environment

A brief summary of what's happening in the environment is that if we don't take urgent action to reduce carbon emissions, life on earth will cease. The planet Earth will still exist, although the devastation created by humans is forecast by scientific evidence to create conditions that make life impossible.

At the 2021 UN Climate Change Conference (COP26), businesses were challenged to defend their actions to alleviate the climate crisis by declaring meaningful action. Organisations are finding themselves subject to changes in buyers' purchasing as a protest to business activities seen as damaging the climate. Disruption to business activities such as blocking deliveries in the supply chain comes from activists such as Extinction Rebellion. 'Greenwashing' is the label given to businesses 'saying all the right things but failing to deliver' (Love and Eccles, 2022).

An International Labour Organization report (2018) identified industry losses:

- Jobs relying on ecosystem services: agriculture, fisheries, forestry, tourism
- Good working conditions rely on the absence of:
  - environmental hazards: storms, air pollution
  - environmental stability: predictable precipitation patterns, constancy of temperatures
- Risks associated with environmental degradation affecting vulnerable workers.

Organisations are now more in the public eye examining the authenticity of business values and sustainability policies; criticism blames, and attempts to shame in accusatory tones that too little is being achieved too slowly. Climate change not only provides the opportunity for collective action, it's essential this happens now. This is a politically advantageous time for organisations to demonstrate social responsibility by uniting in declaring the issues and how to cooperate for a measurable, maintainable and remedial difference.

Business leaders feel pressure to build more sustainable enterprises from key stakeholders (Winston, 2019) and that persists into current times. Customers and employees are cited as the top two vote getters on how they manage sustainability. Millennials and Gen Z (born between 1997 and 2012) are keen to see that companies they work for 'stand for something (having a) higher purpose and mission'. Consumers and customers seek assurances that business is 'done the right way'.

The use of an outfacing 'political agenda' claiming authenticity as a responsible employer is under closer scrutiny as the public, shareholders and employees question the reality of organisational commitment to saving the environment. Pollution worldwide is continuously reported in the media and the call for accountability increases. How might politically astute leaders declare a genuine intention validated by action to align business activities with environmental improvement metrics?

Changes in technology

The commercial market will become more competitive as businesses strive to retain and gain market share and respond to the pace of change and the re-engineering of the working world. Technology now takes centre-stage in business operations. Advances in what's available in automating workplace operations are probably too fast for businesses to remain agile in upgrading in-house technology. I suppose what's helpful is that the challenge imposes indiscriminately! Technological intelligence will be at a premium and reacting to the reported employability power of the younger generations, what will incentivise engagement?

Any organisation digitising its processes can access Artificial Intelligence (AI) for a smoother, faster and more efficient transformation. As long as the data is available, then AI can redefine what can be digitised. This clearly has implications for the future of work. We already have AI accompanying us daily in ways that we may not always be aware of and the signs are that there will be significant impact and life-changing effects in the coming decades. Job roles will become obsolete as AI is adapted and programmed to offer the same if not more efficient productivity.

The World Economic Forum estimates 85 million jobs will be replaced by machines with AI by 2025 – only three years away at the time of writing. AI will change the workplace by helping to make humans faster, more efficient and more productive. The question now is how business can successfully use AI in ways that enables – not replaces – the human workforce. Retraining will be key and casualties will result for those resisting the change.

We can fantasise how the popularity stakes of technology experts will be impacted by organisational politics. Will they become the 'jewel in the crown' of business leaders, will they be the envy of less recognised colleagues jealous of their popularity, or will they vigorously network with other specialists to secure competitive edge for their employer; many options seem likely in the political agenda.

Demographics

The greatest influences on workforce demographics appear to be at opposite ends of the age continuum. As people are becoming generally healthier, life expectancy is being extended. The desire to retire at the 'pensionable' age doesn't seem anywhere near as attractive with entrepreneurial start-ups increasing in this age range. Perhaps a life's ambition being realised when some become more financially stable with less outgoings and more disposable income. A web search offers a range of statistical data depending on the survey size and country of origin. I was fascinated to read a finding claiming that 'In the UK, the average age to start a new business is 40 with an estimated 10,000 businesses started by entrepreneurs over the age of 60.' In the United States, entrepreneur statistics show that the average age to be a successful founder of a start-up company is 45 (Jacimovic, 2021) – no mention of the higher age range. 'Rising energy and food prices – fuelled in part by Russia's invasion of Ukraine blocking flows of agricultural imports and fuel – have elevated inflation around the world' (Halpert, 2022) and may have changed this employment pattern.

Younger workers appear to be seeking employers who demonstrate purpose, integrity and matched values. Demands go beyond a 'quiet dimly-lit capsule' or 'padded rage space' to caring about the environment – after all they're inheriting the climate created by older generations; a green working space including health gardens may become a feature of contemporary working.

Gen Z is defining the new office (*The New York Times*, 2021). Younger people are determining the workplace norms and questioning what they see as the outmoded way of older workers – we may say, so what's new? – this time we're talking about older workers being only slightly older than Gen Z! This includes their views about organisational politics.

Gen Z's demands are higher and they don't hesitate to say what they want. A request now may be wanting to finish the day's work when the daily task list is completed. Remember Gen Z joined the workforce in the midst of a pandemic that disrupted the way we work. This generation has the 'norm' for a way of working not as new – just as is. Recruitment software company RippleMatch found that more than two-thirds of Gen Z surveyed 'wanted a job that will indefinitely stay remote'. Generational frictions are evidently particularly apparent in companies run by and catering to a largely millennial demographic. Gen Z and millennials want different working patterns – no more the late night working that millennials easily adopt along with a shared takeaway, Gen Z wants to set their own hours and protect their health and they're not afraid to make this known and to be in 'defiance of workplace hierarchy'. Gen Z has no problem with delegating tasks to upper-level management. What does this say about employees older than millennials when evidently we're likely to have five generations in the workforce with people retiring later?

So, how might demographics feature in organisational politics in this new world? If individual working becomes the norm and personal needs are satisfied, does this reduce the interest in what happens politically? Do you have the same vision that homeworking reveals? One of work becoming secondary to the strengthening of the nuclear family, not really caring too much about what happens 'out there'. This may be an extreme view when some level of communication is needed to make the work process viable. I just had an image of single pods of employees sending and receiving work assignments into a central database managed by AI and seeing the demise of the workforce as we know it. Science fiction becoming reality?

Two scenarios come readily to mind. The first is that some won't want to engage with organisational politics seen as irrelevant or perhaps intrusive in their newly found freedom and contentment with a new world separated from the bonds of being ensconced in a remote workplace alienating home life. The second is a level of paranoia developing from the 'not knowing what's going on', losing the impetus of why we work and the loss of face-to-face contact creating social isolation and possibly mental health issues. Informal conversations can be the bedrock of 'belonging' and the foundation for finding out 'what's going on' and 'who's who in the influencing network'.

Leaders' response to connecting the organisation with these environmental challenges

So, how will these changes to working practices affect the leadership role? What is certain is that the future of work is uncertain with the level of disturbance influencing the system in which work functions and impacts those who participate in it.

Covid-19, the environment and technology

Agile leadership means reacting to these macro-disrupters by staying ahead of the curve; attempting to forecast preventative measures informed by developments in the system. Scientific data is rich in extrapolating longer-term predictions for contagious viruses similar to coronavirus and of cautionary signs in the direction of travel in the environment. I'm also reminded that scientific predictions are not infallible and the intelligent leader simultaneously remains vigilant to unexpected events.

The politically capable leader will be alert to the possibility of these systemic fluctuations and technological advances and REASON the intelligence of renewing, energising, activating, sustaining and organising mutually supportive networks.

Flexible working

The probability of people preferring solitary working is unlikely when human beings generally have a social need to interact and be relational with others. We are tribal and can become physically and mentally unwell if left in isolation too long.

Online platforms encouraging shorter meetings precipitate screen fatigue and brain fog inciting lack of concentration. Virtual meetings have become common practice and likely to continue as expedient for distributed teams in a range of locations. Shorter meetings essentially encourage focused discussions culminating in increased efficiency – no time we may think for lingering in the political maze.

If office workers are trickling back but most will stay at home (Hurley and Clarence-Smith, 2022), this will inevitably affect the organisation of work. Business and team structures will likely become more fluid. Employees may prefer leaderless working and welcome the responsibility of owning productivity quotients, producing development plans based on recognised skill gaps, ownership of team engagement and shared decision-making. My reflection is the possibility of removing the necessity of a leadership role coordinating productivity and encouraging collaboration between team members and a signal for leaderless self-organising teams.

Flexible working is encouraging and empowering smaller work groups to define how they operate and to be productive when some employers are trying to tempt people back to the office with incentives. Many don't need enticement when 'welcoming screen release and being muted' to once again interact with colleagues.

Clearly, the impact of coronavirus is making the situation difficult to predict as regional variances tell different stories. What might be business as usual in one part of the world with most returning to the workplace may be a different story in another part of the world where infection rates remain high or have forced different working patterns. Difficult to predict the unpredictable when it seems we'll continue to work with the threat of coronavirus or similar. It seems highly probable that some aspect of flexible working will continue at least in the foreseeable future.

The fallout is likely to be that leaders in different sectors will have different challenges. The airline industry at the time of writing is oscillating between capacity growth and staff shortages with coronavirus striking and reducing flight capability leading to more redundancies and staff leaving to find job security elsewhere.

Large cities that have a high proportion of office workers are likely to be greatly affected. Shops that rely on commuter footfall are rapidly losing sales and without robust online shopping experiences may go into liquidation. So, how can leaders inject vitality into these decreasing markets? Relocating to outer-city locations may breathe new life into depressed sales and invigorate the shopping habit of wanting to feel and see the merchandise before purchasing. Those leaders with the ability to acknowledge the trend and be agile in diversification are likely to succeed. Leaders will need to predict what changes are needed in employee profiles – what roles are obsolete possibly through the changes in work brought about by coronavirus and also artificial intelligence. Being politically astute is being skilled at wider networking and gaining intelligence from different sectors by increasing informed contacts and building a broad knowledge base.

What I'm noticing is that pop-up offices are on the increase – office space can be rented by the hour, day, week and longer. There are myriad reasons for this, some of which are already visited. What stands out is that we sometimes want to escape the pressure of being continuously in the workplace – the social interaction mostly welcomed can take over sometimes, especially in a work-space without walls. Teams may want to gather offsite – something about the offsite phenomenon that's so attractive. We know that a change of environment encourages changes in energy and creativity and there is also the 'catchup' time full of speculation and a good 'dose of gossip' – or is this disguised organisational politics: who knows what about who, who's up for promotion, what might be the future of job security, what are leaders not telling us?

Wellbeing of employees and expectations

The healthy workplace is one with a gratifying environment where people are encouraged to push boundaries, overcome challenges and chart purposeful paths in life and work. Even though work has the potential to enhance personal growth and development, it can fall short of these aspirations. Work today is subject to continuous technological change, breakneck deadlines, employee reductions reflecting business reorganisations.

The stress that unhealthy workspaces attract is by nature detrimental to wellbeing. Enlightened leaders realise that wellbeing and mental health impact productivity as does the potential for burnout. Employers do well to remember a duty of care under health and safety legislation.

A CIPD report on Health and Wellbeing at Work (2022) asks if wellbeing is falling off the business agenda. Results confirmed many organisations' accelerated activities on employee health and wellbeing, cementing its position as a top priority on the business agenda. Signs also appear to imply this is waning when there is 'less management focus on health and wellbeing compared with the first year of the pandemic'.

Whilst the apparent family-friendly and life-choice options from homeworking are welcomed by many, this isn't preferred by everyone. I recall several virtual meetings with videos turned off as children, pets and deliveries demanded attention and side conversations about juggling demands being stressful. What has been welcomed is bringing more parts of ourselves to work; calls feel more relaxed and we get more of the sense of the person in their home environment.

A BCG survey (Dahik et al., 2020) states that social connectivity is what enables us to be collaboratively productive, improving communication, increasing efficiency, accelerating skills acquisition, harnessing innovation and reducing absenteeism.

When it comes to promoting good employee health, companies need to focus on both physical health and mental wellbeing. While employees who are no longer commuting have more time to exercise, it is easy for them to be sedentary when working remotely.

A leader's role in wellbeing is one of modelling behaviours that nurture care and counter the negative side of organisational politics:

- notice signs that a team is struggling and explore the cause(s)
- unfair demands underpinned by career-damaging threats actively eradicated
- resist rewarding a 'long hours culture' and penalising those who resist the pressure
- encourage positive work habits that retain staff
- introduce more fun to build resilience, encourage connection and flow (Price, 2022).

Social and psychological capability needed in leaders

Social connectivity

Recreating social connectivity in virtual settings is demanding yet essential and will be even more critical as companies start hiring new employees who have not built social capital from pre-Covid-19 times. The integration of existing and new employees will also benefit from creative solutions where flexible working co-exists with recruitment.

Working relationships have never been more important during these unpredictable times, making versatility in leadership style a vital and observable presence. When the 'going gets really tough', social support is essential for building capacity to bounce back from stressful experiences. Numerous models of leadership are promoted, although there doesn't seem to be one that outshines the rest. My thinking is seeing adaptive leadership as a kaleidoscope of styles giving variety, versatility and vibrancy that brings assurance of steadfastness no matter the speed of each rotation.

Social connections deliver political intelligence; more associations bring more links to wider networks both within and beyond one's immediate circle of contacts. The wider system offers a support structure when internal networks are under pressure and disabling influences erode stamina and resilience.

Key questions for reflective leadership include:

- How confident are you that yours is a culture that nurtures social connectivity practices in your business?
- What arrangements are most effective for bringing together distributed teams?
- What flexible working measures replicate employee engagement that mirrors the corridor meeting and the water cooler circle?
- What fun do you inject into virtual meetings that replaces the informal chat that preceded on-site meetings?
- How effective are you at engaging with positive organisational politics with your team?
- How do you know when damaging organisational politics are present?

Psychological capability

Hall (2020) wrote about today's world of work being less possible to predict risk when operating within a volatile, complex and uncertain environment. Succeeding in today's workplaces is more to do with how well individuals adapt and thrive under enormous pressure than level of intelligence or working extra hard. Two years of coronavirus have probably multiplied this phenomenon, leading to propensity for error; it's more difficult to get things right even when we know failure can provide valuable learnings.

Psychological malfunction clearly impacts leaders' ability to make effective decisions and depending on willingness and aptitude for engaging with healthy or unhealthy organisational politics will determine to what level this capability is affected. What's important is that business leaders become aware of what induces psychological breakdown. To develop the ability to step back, reflect on the situation and intentionally reframe reduces and perhaps eradicates the impact that stress causes on the human nervous system that diminishes high performance.

Is it more politically astute to demonstrate self-restraint and project the image of control under duress or is it healthier to show vulnerability as a leader?

Kegan and Lahey (2009) offer three levels of how we make sense of and operate in the world in profoundly different ways: the socialised mind, the self-authoring mind and the self-transforming mind offer a segue to assess the predictability of future capability and how organisational politics impacts on leaders' functioning ability.

The *socialised mind* is interpreted as being conformist, dependent and dependable; individuals are shaped by shared norms and beliefs. The resulting consistency in action is helpful when emergencies arise and people follow instructions and don't ask questions. Engaging with politics will likely follow a path that people perceive leaders want. People are likely to share vocabulary and use politics as an organisational glue. Not much chance of such an organisation surviving today's turbulent times.

The *self-authoring mind* emerges as individuals mature, become more confident about challenging the status quo; own worldviews are expressed and only reinforcing information is given attention. This approach makes efficient use of time, although lacking awareness of alternative perspectives and what's happening in the wider system is likely to result in missing opportunities and developments that maintain organisational viability. Politics are likely to have a level of complexity. People will want to play at politics with those who have a similar mindset and avoid those that 'don't play the game'.

Elements of the *self-transforming mind* are likely to be more relevant to leaders needing vision for the future. People here work on and not in the business. I find in my practice this essential mode of leading is one that can be neglected. Enterprising clients find time for coaching that offers space to reflect on how the business is operating and what may be essential to notice for the viability of the operation. A space also to identify who's important in decision-making, who will be allies and who are likely to challenge. This is where organisational politics become as complex as the challenges faced by leaders. Who needs to be won over, who will contribute ideas that are transformative, who will deflect opinions that contradict their own. A leader at this level of maturity accepts there are alternative views and welcomes the interjections of others. The organisation cannot remain static to survive in a constantly changing commercial environment. They will look beyond themselves and colleagues and immerse themselves in sense-making of wider issues. The leader with a self-transforming mindset is aware of the value and quality of relationship. They understand their behaviour can encourage and discourage and will calibrate interactions with others to elicit what needs to be done at a meta level to engage appropriate resources. These leaders are emotionally and socially intelligent and maintain a strong focus on the organisational political framework operating within their immediate system and beyond.

A coaching assignment that comes immediately to mind illustrates how reviewing and planning an approach to gain agreement have to be carefully reflected upon to reveal possible hurdles, easily opened doors and who's important to 'get on side'. This executive, engaged in discussions impacting on parliamentary decisions, was able to download fears, recognise areas of value to offer and anticipate areas 'willing to lose' to make sure the critical agenda had a chance of being accepted.

What's needed from our leadership now is a profile more aligned to the 'self-transforming mind' and possibly more. Leaders have to:

- be psychologically fit
- be resilient to the point of elasticity

- be able to self-manage through heightened awareness
- be unafraid of showing vulnerability
- take responsibility for when things don't work out
- include others when things go well
- take creativity and innovation to new levels
- engender trust
- be creators of working in a transformed workplace
- keep calm and cope in turbulent times.

This is leadership about personal attributes overtaking technical skills; it's about continuously adaptive leadership that keeps pace with and anticipates the demands of the growing integrated world in which we do business.

Does the word 'superhuman' come to mind? Of course it does! … and the only compensation is that most leaders face the same challenges although the playing field can be a lonely place – and this is where the positive elements of organisational politics rise to the surface with the acknowledgement it's common sense to get involved.

How to communicate as a politically conscious leader

Goffee and Jones's (2019) text sets out several parameters for communicating when evaluating leadership potential – as a leader, how effectively do you:

- Use the right mode of communication for the message, context, audience?
- Communicate strengths and weaknesses, values and vision?
- Be yourself: use humour and tell stories?
- Listen?

If leaders send emails 24/7, this may influence others to do the same. Taking time to share any positive news or work achievements with colleagues demonstrates inclusivity by keeping everyone informed.

In these unprecedented turbulent times, it's not surprising that we humans are seeking some solace and ways of healing from perceived 'attacks' on our wellbeing. We seek more connection, having reinstated the realisation that we're all connected and individualism isn't actually as productive, therapeutic or as much fun as recognising the value of interdependency that is prevalent in our natural world – and that includes us all!

We seek the chance for happiness, knowing this feeds our wellbeing – so what can leaders do here? What are the soft skills leaders can acquire, knowing that soft skills are actually hard to develop?

Here's the hotbed for organisational politics – who are the authentic people in our circle of engagement? The people we know as honest and who we trust, and who are the people that take our energy and steal our ideas in the guise of feigned interest? What are the relationships that nourish us emotionally and those that are purely functional to finish the task? Does it sound strange for a leader to communicate happiness? Weigh up the benefits when, as mentioned earlier in this chapter, people are becoming more selective about who they work with. Environmentally friendly organisations are sourced as being genuinely caring about people and the world we live in – being politically correct with inauthentic shows of social responsibility are soon detected when the evidence of making a difference isn't espoused in values or in the activities of the business.

What is most concerning is the apparent prevalence of sociopathic leadership. A study published by *Fortune* on business leadership found that '12% of corporate senior leadership displays a range of psychopathic traits, which means psychopathy is up to 12 times more common among senior management than among the general population' (Croom, 2021).

Many psychopathic individuals tend to display traits that are widely associated with effective leadership, such as charisma, persuasiveness and creativity. Psychopaths can often be very successful for this reason, especially if they are high-functioning ones who are able to avoid detection over the long term.

Effectively communicating can be as simple as asking someone how they truly are and don't accept it when they say 'fine' – dig deeper to get the real meaning of 'fine'.

When leaders communicate with genuine intent, the message is in service of others.

Summary and what coaches can do

Leadership for tomorrow has to be adaptive to meet the challenges of a fast-changing world matched with increasingly competitive markets and reduced resources. It has probably never been more important that leaders truly value the people they work with. Up to five different demographic age groups will be working and each will have different expectations of their employer.

The opening section of this chapter offers a leadership profile likely to gain leverage from human capital and aid retention of employees where needed. Basically, leaders gain competitive edge through being a good employer – who doesn't want to work in such organisations? Take a look at the companies listed in Fortune 100 Best Companies to Work For® 2021 (www.Greatplacetowork.com) to access a flavour of what enlightened leaders are offering.

Brené Brown (2022) in her 'Dare to Lead' podcast talks with James Rhee about the transformative power of kindness at work. James believes: 'Creating a culture of kindness at work distributes the joy of problem-solving to everyone, creates a safe environment that unleashes innovation and turns perceived liabilities into assets to create real equity value in every meaning of the word.' What's not to like!

How serious do leaders need to be about organisational politics and how important is the leader's role in being explicit in their approach to organisational politics – is engagement an asset or not? Coaches have a role in supporting clients to make this decision.

What coaches can do

- Ask leaders about their legacy.
- Encourage wellbeing and ask about exercise routines – with homes morphing into an office, people struggle to switch off after work.
- Start sessions with mindfulness practice.
- Work outside for an energising change to an office environment using nature as an effective counterbalance to – phones can be effective with a good signal and when working in person isn't practical.
- Explore with clients during the contracting conversation the level of intent for genuinely seeking change and willingness to act on development areas in leadership.
- Self-reflect to determine how authentic we're being as coaches to avoid co-dependency and colluding with clients assuaging their guilt at 'developmental avoidance' (Clutterbuck, 2022).

The following end-of-chapter offering from practice illustrates how being overly authentic as a leader can sometimes be politically dangerous in a competitive environment. Being politically astute is having awareness of what to say, when and to whom, embraced by ethical principles.

A client happened to mention, 'You know it's the political piece.' The phrase seems disjointed with the topic. As the session was supporting the client's impact on organisational leaders with the possibility of being a career influencer, I asked if we could revisit the 'political piece'. Data being shared by everyone at the meeting was likely to be manipulated by some was the client's perception, naively crafted by others and expressed frankly by my client as demonstrating authenticity. I reflected on this and accepted the invitation from the client to make observations about the proposed presentation. It was indeed authentic and in places with potential for perhaps over-revealing. Was this the intention – was the self-deprecatory language used as evidence that a feedback report hadn't been massaged to show the client in an overly positive light? In that moment I offered to be 'the audience' watching the presentation, listening to this self-reveal, offering possible reactions and asking for the client's reactions. The rehearsal enabled the client to reflect and decide to create a preamble to the presentation explaining how tough it had been to have blind spots revealed and how working with a coach had provided the space to work through patterns of behaviour that had undermined the intended leadership style. Lessons had been hard learned in understanding impact on others and to undo years of creating a style believed to be the one needed and adopted through being raised in a family of perfectionists.

References

Brown, B. (2022) Kindness, math, and the power of goodwill with James Rhee, *Dare to Lead* [podcast], 28 March. Available at: https://bit.ly/3JI5lqm.

CIPD (2022) *Health and wellbeing at work*, CIPD Survey Report in partnership with Simplyhealth, April. Available at: https://www.cipd.co.uk/Images/health-wellbeing-work-report-2022_tcm18-108440.pdf.

Clutterbuck, D. (2022) *Coaching and Mentoring: A journey through the models, theories, frameworks and narratives of David Clutterbuck*. London: Routledge, pp. 38–47.

Croom, S. (2021) 12% of corporate leaders are psychopaths. It's time to take this problem seriously, *Fortune*, 6 June. Available at: https://fortune.com/2021/06/06/corporate-psychopaths-business-leadership-csr/.

Dahik, A., Lovich, D., Kreafle, C., Bailey, A., Kilmann, J., Kennedy, D., Roongta, P., Schuler, F., Tomlin, L. and Wenstrup, J. (2020) *What 12,000 employees have to say about the future of remote work*, Boston Consulting Group, 11 August. Available at: https://www.bcg.com/publications/2020/valuable-productivity-gains-covid-19.

Frost, G. (2022) What are my rights to flexible working?, *The Times Money Mentor*, 26 July [updated 6 December].

Goffee, R. and Jones, G. (2019) *Why Should Anyone Be Led by You?* Boston, MA: Harvard Business Review Press.

Hall, B. (2020) Teaching corporate resilience to tomorrow's leaders, *Forbes*, 7 May. Available at: https://www.forbes.com/sites/forbescoachescouncil/2020/05/07/teaching-corporate-resilience-to-tomorrows-leaders/?sh=3bc1b69c17f1.

Halpert, M. (2022) Inflation goes global: It's not just rising in the U.S. – but Europe, South Korea and more, *Forbes*, 23 June. Available at: https://www.forbes.com/sites/madelinehalpert/2022/06/23/inflation-goes-global-its-not-just-rising-in-the-us-but-europe-south-korea-and-more/?sh=585374a24e2f.

Hurley, J. and Clarence-Smith, L. (2022) Office workers trickle back but most still stay at home, *The Times*, 18 February. Available at: https://www.thetimes.co.uk/article/office-workers-trickle-back-but-most-still-stay-at-home-hrskrhh87.

International Labour Office (ILO) (2018) *The employment impact of climate change adaptation*. Input Document for the G20 Climate Sustainability Working Group. Available at: https://www.ilo.org/global/topics/green-jobs/WCMS_645572/lang--en/index.htm.

Jacimovic, D. (2021) 27 UK entrepreneur statistics to inspire you, *The Circular Board*, 26 April. Available at: https://thecircularboard.com/entrepreneur-statistics/.

Kegan, R. and Lahey, L. (2009) *Immunity to Change: How to overcome it and unlock potential in yourself and your organization*. Boston, MA: Harvard Business Press

Love, C. and Eccles, R.G. (2022) How leaders can move beyond greenwashing toward real change, *Harvard Business Review*, 25 January. Available at: https://hbr.org/2022/01/how-leaders-can-move-beyond-greenwashing-toward-real-change.

Price, C. (2022) *The Power of Fun: Why fun is the key to a happy and healthy life*. London: Bantam Press.

The New York Times (2021) Gen Z is defining the new office: Why bosses in their late 30s are afraid of the 20-somethings who work for them, *The Economic Times*, last updated 12 November. Available at: https://economictimes.indiatimes.com/magazines/panache/gen-z-is-defining-the-new-office-why-37-somethings-are-afraid-of-the-20-somethings-who-work-for-them/articleshow/87658567.cms?from=mdr.

The Times (2022) Working from home is now a permanent fixture, say bosses, *The Times*, 11 February. Available at: https://www.thetimes.co.uk/article/working-from-home-is-now-a-permanent-fixture-say-bosses-0ldzvm99d.

Winston, A. (2019) What 1,000 CEOs really think about climate change and inequality, *Harvard Business Review*, 24 September. Available at: https://hbr.org/2019/09/what-1000-ceos-really-think-about-climate-change-and-inequality.

10 The Organisational Politics Awareness Tool

By the whole team

There are a number of tools available which allow people to assess their own political astuteness or political skills. One, the multidimensional Political Skill Inventory (PSI), was developed by Gerald Ferris and his colleagues (2005a). The PSI is made up of 18 items that are rated from 'strongly agree' to 'strongly disagree'. It is based on the authors' own framework that we discussed in Chapter 2. It is available as a free download from: https://www.politicalskillat-work.com/.

Ferris and his co-authors have worked on the validation of this tool and reported that their measurement of political skill was positively related to self-monitoring, political savvy and emotional intelligence, and negatively related to trait anxiety. Also, the PSI predicted performance ratings of managers in two samples (Ferris et al., 2005b). In addition, Jacobson and Viswesvaran (2017) found the PSI to have high reliability.

Although this is clearly a valuable and high-quality tool, we have our reservations about the category of 'apparent sincerity', which doesn't feel in line with the concept of high-integrity politics that we find useful. Two of the items that assess apparent sincerity perhaps reflect our concerns: the first is 'It is important that people believe I am sincere in what I say and do', and the second is 'I try to show a genuine interest in other people'. The first of these in particular feels overly conscious and complex to us rather than simply focusing on being sincere.

One of the items for the area of 'networking ability' is: 'At work, I know a lot of important people and am well connected'. It may come down to small nuances of language and cultural differences but again this feels that it might not represent the authenticity which we believe is part of effective political engagement. Despite these minor reservations, the significant development, research and validation efforts of Ferris et al. are highly impressive.

Jean Hartley and colleagues (2013) also developed a skills assessment based on their own 50-item political skills framework; however, it does not seem to be available at present.

The Organizational Savvy Multi-Rater Assessment is based on Rick Brandon and Marty Seldman's *Survival of the Savvy* (2004), which we discussed in Chapter 2 and uses their concept of organisational savvy. This is a 65-item rating instrument that yields an overall Organizational Savvy score and 13 separate Skill Set scores. Participants are rated as 'proficient', 'capable' or 'vulnerable' for each skill set. The multi-rater element of this assessment adds value and it provides a comparison of self-ratings versus ratings of managers, direct reports, colleagues and customers. There is also the opportunity for raters to make text comments.

There is no information shared about the validity or reliability of this tool, but for those who find the framework useful it is an interesting source of data and would provide valuable material for reflecting on with a coach or mentor. The assessment is commercially available from Brandon Partners at: https:// brandonpartners.com/organizational-savvy-multi-rater-assessment/.

While working on this book, we looked at the different assessment tools available and saw the potential to do something a little different. We did not aim to design an assessment tool that would make claims to be reliable or valid. We were more interested in preparing a simple free tool that people can use on their own or with a coach or mentor. Our aim was to support reflection and to challenge participants on their views about organisational politics and their own competencies.

We prepared an initial version of the tool and shared it with a wide network of people. Based on their feedback we made some revisions. One of the suggestions made was to include a definition of organisational politics in the tool. In a deliberate attempt to make it simple, we included a definition of organisational politics that aims to maintain the neutrality of politics as a behaviour:

> *The use or abuse of formal or informal power and influence to achieve objectives that may be overt or covert.*

Our aim is not to measure but to raise awareness. We also want to encourage people's reflection on their own approach to organisational politics. We use five different categories of political competencies and also aim to capture some beliefs about politics. We think these represent many common approaches, and we also want to suggest ways people can develop high-integrity political behaviours.

To use the tool, people tick boxes if they agree with a statement. The boxes are arranged in columns indicating the five categories we have focused on. There is a risk that this format can lead people's answers in a certain direction as they try to understand the meaning behind each column. In future, this might be improved by putting the tool on a simple website so that participants simply agree or disagree with each statement and then get a final result. We also aim to provide some interpretive guidance on assessing the scores and also some follow-up reflection questions.

Again, we would like to emphasise that our Organisational Politics Awareness Tool makes no claims to be a valid scientific instrument. We do believe (and have had this belief reinforced by those who have used the tool) that this is a useful support to reflection. We see this as an ideal tool to use as part of a coaching or mentoring engagement. Coaches and mentors can also complete it themselves, to understand better their own views about organisational politics.

We offer this as a starting point for reflection and dialogue. We would also encourage practitioners to modify or expand the tool so that it best meets their own needs and cultural context.

References

Brandon, R. and Seldman, M. (2004) *Survival of the Savvy: High-integrity political tactics for career and company success*. New York: Simon & Schuster.

Ferris, G., Davidson, S. and Perrewé, P. (2005a) *Political Skill at Work: Impact on work effectiveness*. Mountain View, CA: Davies-Black.

Ferris, G., Treadway, D., Kolodinsky, R., Hochwarter, W., Kacmar, C., Douglas, C. and Frink, D. (2005b) Development and validation of the Political Skill Inventory, *Journal of Management*, 31 (1): 126–152.

Hartley, J., Alford, J., Hughes, O. and Yates, S. (2013) *Leading with political astuteness – a white paper*. Open Research Online. Available at: https://oro.open.ac.uk/38471/1/__userdata_documents2_bar2_Desktop_Leading_with_political_astuteness_white_paper_2013.pdf.

Jacobson, R.K. and Viswesvaran, C. (2017) A reliability generalization study of the Political Skill Inventory, *SAGE Open*, 7 (2). Available at: https://doi.org/10.1177/2158244017706714.

The Organisational Politics Awareness Tool

This tool aims to prompt reflection and help identify the areas in which you could further develop your political astuteness.

Definition of Organisational Politics
The use or abuse of formal or informal power and influence to achieve objectives that may be overt or covert.

Your Assumptions
Read through the following statements and place a tick in the appropriate box (if the statement is true or false for you).

	True	False
Organisational politics are harmful and should be avoided		
Organisational politics can be both beneficial and harmful and are a normal part of organisational management		

Diagnostic Questions
Place a tick in the white box next to the statements you agree with and then add up the number of ticks in each column.

	Column 1	Column 2	Column 3	Column 4	Column 5
I sometimes find myself outmanoeuvred by people who are more adept at politics than I am					
I can usually work out the motivations of other people					
I often feel powerless because I have little or no influence on decisions that affect me or my team					
I encourage members of the team to raise problems and tough issues					
I see value in networking beyond my immediate team					

	Column 1	Column 2	Column 3	Column 4	Column 5
I know how to use other people's hidden agendas to achieve what I want			☐		
I collaborate regularly with colleagues across the organisation to learn about working practices that influence operations in my area of responsibility					☐
I believe that recognition comes from doing your job well	☐				
I am good at convincing other people of my ideas or to follow me		☐			
I encourage colleagues to be open about their mistakes				☐	
I bring both personal and organisational values into context when making difficult decisions		☐			
I seek out and build relationships with the real decision-makers, wherever they are					☐
I seek out diverse perspectives and value dissenting opinions				☐	
I can turn other people's self-interest to my advantage			☐		
I make time to encourage exchange of information with stakeholders likely to be impacted by decisions made in my sphere of influence					☐

	Column 1	Column 2	Column 3	Column 4	Column 5
I spend little time networking	☐				
I can be selective in the data I present, in order to support the argument that I want to make			☐		
I am good at helping others find acceptable compromises		☐			
I confront political game-playing by providing well-timed, evidence-based interventions				☐	
I consult with colleagues and stakeholders beyond my immediate circle to gain a sense of their preferred options before a decision-making meeting					☐
I see myself as a champion of information dissemination that informs organisational and leadership development					☐
I am good at helping others contrast short-term and long-term outcomes of decisions		☐			
I switch off and disengage when I see people playing political games	☐				
I promote transparency in decision-making and actively share information with the team				☐	
I enjoy the feeling of getting my own way			☐		

	Column 1	Column 2	Column 3	Column 4	Column 5
I promote strong team cohesion by role-modelling fairness and inclusivity				☐	
I feel uncomfortable about engaging in self-promotion	☐				
I build a network of influencers inside and outside the organisation to inform future business operations and strategy					☐
I don't feel the need to share my private agenda with colleagues			☐		
I consciously build relationships with people at work		☐			
My personal success is very important to me			☐		
I am intentional about fostering a climate of trust and respect where people feel appreciated and valued				☐	
I build alliances with colleagues so that we can all achieve our goals in the organisation		☐			
When I sense office politics at work, I keep my head down and get on with my job	☐				
I use social media for essential knowledge gathering and sharing					☐
I discourage the attitude of 'knowledge is power'				☐	
I have a strong awareness of personal risk			☐		

	Column 1	Column 2	Column 3	Column 4	Column 5
I create the climate where people can share their opinions with more senior people				✓	
I will adapt my behaviour to get on with powerful people			✓		
I don't feel comfortable using power and influence in my organisation	✓				
I have a strong network of people at all levels, who I can rely on for support when needed		✓			
I think about where power lies in the wider system and how I need to engage with it to achieve organisational goals					✓
I can usually build good rapport with people		✓			
I will do what it takes to achieve my goals			✓		
I think my business results should speak for themselves	✓				
Total number of statements you agree with in each column (add number of ticks)					

Understanding Your Score

- Write down the number of statements you agree with in each column in the shaded fields below, and refer to the score guide to understand what your score means.

Column	Corresponding Category	Score	High/Medium/Low
Column 1	Political Naivety		
Column 2	Manages Politics with Authenticity		
Column 3	Uses Politics for Personal Gain		
Column 4	Influences the Political Landscape		
Column 5	Engages with the Wider Political System		

Score Guide	
7–9	High
4–6	Medium
1–3	Low

Both a high score and a low score can be optimal, depending on the category. Read through the explanations below to understand how you could further develop your political astuteness.

Political Naivety – If you score highly here, it is worth reflecting on your assumptions about organisational politics. Seeing them as neutral rather than bad, and thinking about how you might be more actively engaged with power, while maintaining your integrity, may be helpful for you.

Manages Politics with Authenticity – If you score low here, think about how you can develop skills that will help you engage with others more with integrity.

Uses Politics for Personal Gain – A high score here indicates that you have a win/lose attitude to power and are prepared to sacrifice others to achieve your goals. In an environment where we have ongoing relationships with others and increasing transparency, ask yourself how ethical and sustainable this is? How do you want to be known in the organisation? How can you develop a more collaborative approach and still achieve your goals?

Influences the Political Landscape – If you score low or medium on this, think about how you can shape the environment you work in to make it a healthier place for everyone. Which of these behaviours could you adopt in future?

Engages with the Wider Political System – If you score highly here, you clearly have a strong sense of engagement with the wider environment of power and influence. If not, would it be worthwhile for you to try some of these behaviours?

Reflections
Reflect on the questions below and if appropriate share your thoughts with someone else.

What have you learned about yourself?

What would you like to change or develop further?

What actions would you like to take forward, if any?

What are other reflections, if any?

Appendix 1: Overview of supplementary survey responses

Profile of secondary survey interviewees

1 Senior Partner, Big 4 Accounting firm, Cyprus
2 HR Director, South America
3 CEO, Public Sector Organisation, UK
4 Partner, Head of UK Indirect Tax

Q1: What's your definition of organisational politics?

HR Director, South America

- They are part of the culture, although you can't see them clearly; they're used like self-serving behaviours and involve the use of power and social networking.
- They also work for the benefit of the organisation, although mostly to try to protect the individual as people realise it's not possible to do 'your own thing'.
- I think politics give order.

Q2: When you reflect on politics in an organisation and you think about gender issues, what are your first thoughts?

Senior Partner, Big 4 Accounting firm, Cyprus

- Expressed a strong aversion to, even hating, organisational politics.
- Politics has no place in organisations as it prevents people being authentic and violates individual values.
- Being transparent and fair is naïve and unrealistic.
- Individuals have to fit with the 'company profile' that undermines diversity and inclusion encouraging different people with different opinions.

HR Director, South America

- It's difficult for women to use their feminine power; intelligence, female attributes that could benefit the company.
- It's about culture and what we need as women; are men conscious of the conditions we operate in?

- I never saw I had a problem as a woman in a company, although I coach loads of women who think they are having issues because they are women.
- We are losing honesty because we have to be 'politically correct' and it's difficult to understand perspectives in every culture.

CEO, Public Sector Organisation, UK

- The organisation (national public sector) isn't the healthiest system in terms of organisational politics. When mention was made of discriminatory behaviour, the response was 'there's no way anyone's going to get rid of him ... he's the golden boy because he's done all the right things in terms of relationships with people up the line and ... maybe I was a bit naïve, I knew there were people acting against me with people on the side-lines throwing in grenades'.
- I suppose my naivety was thinking that doing the right thing and getting people doing the right thing would be enough; my learning is you've got to be more active in neutralising people who are actively working against you and describing you as challenging and difficult because you were prepared to have the difficult conversations.
- I wasn't feeling very resilient; even the people you think are on your side cannot be relied on for support when things get difficult.

Partner, Head of UK Indirect Tax

- Is it ever a good thing if the person holding the power has good ideas; can the organisational politics be used for good – as it's usually used for bad, isn't it?

Q3: How do you think politics may or may not impact on women?

Senior Partner, Big 4 Accounting firm, Cyprus

- The organisation is male-dominated with male language and norms carried into business meetings that excludes women as the men 'stick together' and seek the same profile for promotions or allocation of assignments; it is therefore difficult for women to play organisational politics even if they wished to.
- Speaking out led to a 'big disappointment' in professional life through being honest as the feedback suggestion of being willing to show vulnerability wasn't well received; the result was being overlooked for promotion and exclusion as a senior executive and a realisation that confronting a leadership style was a mistake.
- The learning about speaking out being less than well received was to 'wake up' and be aware of expected behaviour.
- Politics exist when psychological safety is low and inclusion is low on the agenda.

- Although the conversations weren't extensive, there was a sense of 'duty' to the younger generation in drawing attention to the imbalance in the conversation.
- There is very low psychological safety at senior level, so people have a fear of speaking up to avoid different opinions and disagreements; this goes right to the heart of company culture.

HR Director, South America

- Men who wish to continue having power and hold on to information will avoid working with a female personal assistant.
- I was one woman amongst twelve men and one tried to destroy me because I was going too fast; however, he lost his power because he lost his focus.
- It's very rare to find a woman in an executive committee.
- Ideas can be undermined if men feel threatened by a woman.
- Negotiating in a male-dominated environment can be tough because of the gender differences when communicating; men appear tougher, less trusting, use emotive language and don't like to 'lose face'.
- Women have the choice to leave if they wish.
- It's hard for a lot of women (to challenge organisational politics) because it means disruption in ourselves – we have to stand up for what we believe in and there's risk in doing this – especially if you're responsible for bringing an income to support the family and the person being challenged is responsible for your pay award.
- Power is held by a very small group.
- People aren't allowed to use their personal power to take decisions and to show their point of view, although I see signs of this changing as people are starting to seek more spirituality (not religious).

CEO, Public Sector Organisation, UK

- Gender issues of being a female working with white middle-class men as counterparts who were not all accepting of a female in a CEO role.
- He was like a chameleon saying whatever he thought people wanted to hear and moved from meeting to meeting saying the exact opposite. He learned a strategy of abdicating responsibility and gave himself a very low sense of control and agency.
- How could I as a woman possibly be the preferred candidate? [for the CEO role] Rumours were spread suggesting an affair because I couldn't possibly be doing that job on merit.
- The whole thing about male power and the idea I couldn't possibly be doing that job because I was the best person – all this played out at that time which was quite, quite, difficult.

- The only way I could take control was to get out of this situation (and to leave).
- I felt battered, I was feeling fed up in terms of just the nonsense in terms of the behaviour of others in the system.
- I was asked to do something that 'crossed the line', which didn't sit well with me.
- Internal politics can get caught up with national politics. This has a double edge with you being in the middle, not knowing what's going on in the background, conversations that are either directly shared with you or innuendo – how do you manage to operate in that climate?
- I was completely manipulated and ended up having to leave. It still amazes me how some people will act in a way that you wouldn't contemplate; this still surprises me.
- The only time I went to … was to be shouted at by the person two tiers above me in the organisation. I got this physical reaction when going to … : how crazy is that?
- Male-to-male tends to be more competitive.
- I had quite a few experiences where a woman who wanted to be an alpha female was very threatened by other women who perhaps challenged her status.
- I think the male-to-female plays out in different ways as does the age group.
- It's fair game in terms of trying it on and people think it's okay; I remember my dress being commented on and how the colour suited me – you wouldn't say that about a man's suit would you? This plays into the power dynamic as if this is how a serious conversation starts, it can be hard as a woman to regain that ground; you feel you're automatically starting the conversation at a disadvantage.
- If you're in a toxic system, then people who aren't necessarily bad people behave really badly and I think women are pushed to do that.
- If you're in this place, to some extent you're just being the loudspeaker for the pressure that's coming from above.

Partner, Head of UK Indirect Tax

- How things have changed or have they? – where people use their influence for their own self-interest and how I've navigated myself through this over the years and had to give up certain things by doing that.
- I'm very conscious of who's in the inner circle and make a conscious decision to be in the middle circle – I don't want to be in the outer ring. I don't want to rock the boat and definitely don't want to be in the inner circle.
- I've given up some positions and could have been bolder to be in the inner circle as I know exactly how to do it – I really don't want to be

there as particularly as a woman I'm just going to be used as a pawn in that inner circle – the token woman.

- I realised how quickly I could be 'trampled to death' in the inner circle – I gave up some of my moral values by doing this as I wasn't speaking out – this is why it exists because it coerces everyone to comply.
- 17% of women are in executive positions in this organisation.
- I walked into a room of 11 men and me – there was lots of jostling, shouting and posturing. One of these men said to me, 'it's alright for you as you're a woman, everyone knows who you are and the reason we do all this jostling is because we're trying to get known.' How many women have used our uniqueness to our advantage – wear brighter colours and more jewellery?
- What was all this about 'it's alright for you'? Was this resentment because the man had to make more effort to get known? Whether it's a good or bad reason on his political compass, it was easier to be a woman?
- Our current CEO has an agenda and one of these areas is Diversity and Inclusion and he wants a leadership legacy to increase numbers of senior people in these groups and fairness in development. May be self-interest but ultimately it's for the good of everyone – can be positive if the person with the power wants a good thing.
- Women don't play and like to be in the middle circle and safe but we're negatively affected by it.
- Where it affected my career is not to be able to speak out because if I do, I'm perceived to be emotional – I've had this perception confirmed.
- Is speaking out worth it when I get penalised? Over the years, I've only spoken up if it's important to me and self-fulfilling prophecy is that I am emotional. It's something in our biology that men won't understand.
- Took my courage to broach a subject in a logical, well-thought-through way – he knew it was coming so he went into defence which was attack – it was an emotional outburst and you're supposed to use good judgement and those type of attributes. I did agree I was emotional as the situation warranted it. The outcome was receiving a mail congratulating the way I responded to feedback – for him the script was: I won that then; for men, it is about winning. I obviously didn't say thank you, I just ignored it.
- Put-down language – stuff that is true about women, the language that's used somehow has negative connotations about emotion.
- Balance of power shifts only when there are more women in position. Margaret Thatcher wasn't the best role model that helped women be seen as they are.
- A female CEO was described as fluffy – she didn't succeed – when a woman is an ambassador for women's rights, they're perceived as fluffy or hippy or activist or feminist. When a man brought in the same activities, the action was described as 'how refreshing'.

- Things haven't changed enough – we don't elevate ourselves and don't advocate for one another whereas men do – it's inherent – they go out after work, play golf, have a curry and the men promote each other for various projects and positions – women go home to look after the children.
- Are organisational politics going to exist until the end of time? If senior people have good intentions, they can drive the change. In the post-Covid world, previous barriers aren't there: staying at work late, golfing, etc. Are things going to be easier to navigate?
- Experiencing the menopause feels very lonely – being just one person experiencing this in a number of men – why don't I say something? – mention I've lost my mojo – experiencing imposter syndrome. Menopause can be treated as a joke – insensitive and lack of education about menopause.
- We can't say these issues don't affect us because I've always championed women. We have to educate ourselves about what women go through every single day – it's for everyone to start to understand.
- I'm a women leader and the results of a psychometric tell me I still have a preference for men to be a leader – unconscious bias and the way we're socialised. I still unconsciously think men should be a leader – how do you break that? It takes generations. Consciously I make sure I don't do this and unconsciously I think I do.

Q4: I'm wondering what can we do as women to address situations where we perceive we're unable to have an authentic conversation?

Senior Partner, Big 4 Accounting firm, Cyprus

- Societal norms relating to gender need challenging so that both men and women are treated fairly; men progress more quickly and further than women – we have a 'blocked not leaky pipeline' for women's career progression.
- Men are needed as 'allies' to initiate change along with 'unconscious bias' training.
- Some allies already exist alongside some cynics too who view equality, diversity and inclusion as 'fluffy stuff' with 'too much time spent on this'; therefore, focus on the people who are allies.
- Make this a mainstream leadership meeting rather than squeezed into an already busy agenda.

HR Director, South America

- We need to learn to manage our power: to feel free to say what we think, sharing our points of view, and knowing and feeling our limits, to respect them. Also to feel and respect the limits of the others.

CEO, Public Sector Organisation, UK

- I'm quite good at getting into the hidden dynamics and identifying what's really going on in a room; I think I'm quite emotionally intelligent as well.
- I think I was quite good at calling out bad behaviours but probably didn't do it enough when resilience was low; there's a wonderful phrase, 'don't bleed in the water with sharks'.
- I trusted people I shouldn't have trusted, so it becomes a spiral going from being fierce in a positive way in terms of calling it out and feeling awful to feeling powerless. It took me 18 months to get over the grief (of this experience) and move on.
- A good diversionary tactic is to keep busy and deal with whatever comes along the way.
- People who want to be true to themselves and don't fit with the anticipated 'stereotypical norm' end up being penalised one way or another.
- I think there are massive benefits to being politically astute; it's about using the hidden dynamics in the organisation and using power. You can either use that negatively for self-interest or in a positive way.
- Create energy for change; use internal politics by socialising ideas, getting to people and finding out who the powerful people are and making sure you know they're on your side before going into a formal meeting.
- Create consensus behind what you think is the right action and to some extent compromising and not thinking you always have the right answer; compromise when you think you're swimming against the flow.
- Women are more emotionally intelligent than men and as we move into more complex, multi-layered organisations with distributed leadership, I feel very positive the time is right for the female style of leadership to come into its own.
- Women can be more supportive of each other and just because you're doing well doesn't mean somebody else has to do badly. I think I was brought up in this sort of dominant culture at the time which is, in order to shine, somebody else has to 'fall off a cliff'.
- We want someone to 'have our back' and this is what I'd want to be for other women.
- It's no good us thinking, making the assumption that all men are political when we're talking about gender.
- Don't be afraid of politics and use it with positive intent; internal and cross-organisational politics can actually be a really helpful tool in levering change.
- On the dark side, ignoring politics isn't always the right strategy; I think there's something about actually challenging and calling out where people are using politics very negatively and for self-interest.
- You need to be in a position of power to call it out.

Partner, Head of UK Indirect Tax

- You have to find your way through organisational politics – you give up a part of you to do this, or worse, give up time with school children – tangible stuff by playing this game and compromise to pay the mortgage.
- Women who behave like men aren't helpful.

Q5: Given this action focuses on 'women at the top', what level in the organisation do you think is most affected by politics?

Senior Partner, Big 4 Accounting firm, Cyprus

- The issue is throughout the organisation, including trainees expressing a 'need to adjust and fit', to be like men, including what to wear and behaviour such as understanding the jokes and football.

HR Director, South America

- It depends on the culture: I knew companies that the limitations began in the middle levels, just when a woman showed her ambition. In others, in high positions, if men felt threatened by her power.

Q6: Is there any other impact on women that it has, rather than having to fit into this box? What else does it do to remain?

Senior Partner, Big 4 Accounting firm, Cyprus

- I knew I was being excluded and things were done behind my back. It makes me feel sad to play the game to get the result needed for the company.
- Different patterns of behaviour were noticed in different countries who embraced inclusion more readily mainly because they had more women on the board; you can see the difference when the leaders are women – if you're a minority, you're always cautious about what you say and how you behave.
- Women need a voice without fear of repercussion or not being believed and this means many women speaking up in the same way as the 'Me Too' movement. We need to keep raising awareness about issues that treat some less favourably than others – this includes both men and women.
- Change comes slowly and allies are needed to support this.

HR Director, South America

- The other is a woman´s fear: Being more than their husbands, earning more than them, not taking care of the family enough if they work …

Appendix 2: Fifteen helpful questions

David, in particular, collects powerful questions – ones that stimulate different or deeper thinking in a coaching client. The examples below are some of those that coaches have found especially helpful.

1 Who are the key players in this situation?
2 What are their overt and covert motivations?
3 What will make them consider you/your team as a key part of their strategy?
4 What resources and skills do you have that they will find useful in achieving their objectives?
5 What have you done/could you do to make them aware of you/your team as a politically strategic resource?
6 What core values do you want to uphold, regardless of pressures from others?
7 How can you establish boundaries around values without creating enemies?
8 What resources do you have and what can you do, to get advance warning of politically motivated change?
9 What resources can you muster to block damaging, politically motivated change?
10 When would be the best time to have those resources in place? When would be too late?
11 How much in credit is your 'favour bank'?
12 How clear are you about the intent (purpose) of your boss? Your boss's boss? Key colleagues?
13 How can you ensure you are aware of the undercurrents in the organisation?
14 What principles will you not let go of?
15 Who are your champions and supporters? How are you keeping them motivated to support you?

Appendix 3: Case studies

Case study 1: Taking a political risk

Organisational context

The organisation is a consumer goods company based in the UK making specialist seasonal products. They provide products via their own store network and also via clients, such as department stores and grocery chains. These clients are dependent on this specialist firm providing expertise on the best way to market products to their customers to ensure maximum coverage and interest.

It is a well-established organisation with an employee population with medium to long tenure, from the local area, mostly in their late thirties and forties, who tend to focus on their individual work remits and observe hierarchical boundaries. With the recent coronavirus pandemic, there has been a reactive shift to considering virtual sales in response to customer demand. The approach to marketing tends to focus on tried-and-tested methods.

The individual sharing her story – Serena – joined the organisation on a six-month contract, into a team that managed sales and merchandising for large client accounts. Serena was a recent graduate at the time and saw this as an opportunity to gain experience of a workplace, explore ideas and build relationships.

Situation

Serena was part of a team that managed a national client with hundreds of stores across the UK. Serena's specific project focused on a seasonal product, with marketing work starting three months in advance. Serena's work remit involved administrative tasks which were necessary, albeit dull and repetitive.

Serena's longer-term goal was to have more impact on the marketing for products sold through this client. Realising that she needed advocates to do this, Serena invested time in building relationships with key stakeholders such as the head of social media, marketing technical experts and others through coffee chats on a regular basis. She built relationships and learnt more about the dynamics of the business by asking questions. She explains that this meant that when she had a new idea for using social media for her client account, 'I had a bank of people … and I could offer them a reciprocal opportunity. … In terms of politics at that stage, I knew I couldn't do it on my own, I needed some people to help me do it, already from the start I was trying to build that network.'

Serena made a request to her team to get a budget to launch social media posts for her project with the retail client account. This had not been done before and her team manager and colleagues were not supportive, and she was advised that there was no interest, appetite or budget to do this.

Serena eventually managed to deliver the social media project by mobilising internal resources with no additional corporate spending. This was partly due to the network of advocates that Serena had generated with key stakeholders.

The outcomes from the social media posts were a significant sales uplift, all of the seasonal products sold out across the country, and this was achieved at zero additional costs to the organisation. With such strong results, Serena expected recognition and attention from her bosses. Unfortunately, this was not the case, nor was there any discussion about sharing the results more widely, along with lessons learned. Serena managed her own 'thank-yous' to her stakeholder network.

Early in Serena's time at the company, she had responded to a general invitation from the Managing Director (MD) to join a lunch meeting. Serena had signed up to attend and was the most junior colleague to do so. No other team members wanted to attend and they were surprised that she did. Serena's manager joined the lunch after learning that Serena would be attending. At the lunch, the MD had made an open offer of a one-to-one meeting with anyone who wanted to share updates or discuss ideas.

Now that she was frustrated with the lack of recognition for her project work, Serena took up the standing invite from the MD and requested a meeting. Serena's aim wasn't to get praise for herself but to explain this new approach to working with clients, which she believed represented a significant business opportunity for additional sales and consumer engagement. The MD told Serena to set up an appointment through her Personal Assistant (PA).

Again, Serena was aware of building the relationship with the MD's PA and was persistent to make sure the meeting actually happened even though it was rescheduled twice.

When they met, the MD was extremely positive about what Serena had done and the business opportunity. The MD asked Serena to share the activity and results at the next company townhall, which had 1,200 colleagues attending. This was a big deal for Serena as such a junior and new employee in the company. At that presentation Serena explained the project and the teamwork that had been involved in achieving the success.

As a result, Serena's line manager and the Sales Director took greater interest in Serena and her ideas and also changed their attitude and approach to trying new things, whereas historically the team had demonstrated resistance to change.

Serena's reflections on the case

As she reflected on the case, Serena was very conscious of the different power relationships within the organisation and the need for her to build allies, manage potential blockers and work to engage with people across the organ-isation to achieve her goals. She describes herself as someone who does reflect on people and relationships more than many of her new graduate peers.

Because she knew that she would only be with the company for six months, Serena notes that this might have made her braver than otherwise. She didn't have the support as an ally of her own boss or their boss, but still wanted to raise awareness of the success of the project she had worked on. She took the risk of circumnavigating them to bring senior management's attention to the work she had done. She noted that 'if I had been staying there longer term, I might have been a bit more careful about some of the characters'.

As a result, she believes that the company became more open to experiment-ing with new ideas and to listening more actively to suggestions from more junior employees in the company.

Political learnings and outcomes

We think that Serena's experience of overcoming resistance to change was due to:

Personal attitude and commitment – Serena was keen to get the most from her six-month contract with this company and was very aware of the need to proactively build relationships and drive change to make things happen. She was persistent and prepared to take calculated risks to achieve her goals which were aligned to the organisation's aims.

Building strong stakeholder relationships – with colleagues outside of her team, with the MD and other senior colleagues. Not aligning too closely to any particular group meant that Serena could build a wide and varied network.

Advocacy – having senior sponsors enabled Serena to gain support from her line manager and teams for new ideas, discussions and specifically support from the middle layer of management.

Results – the social media posts resulted in a strong outcome, which reflected well on the whole team. Sharing success built trust and support from other colleagues. The team became more open to change, which supported greater future success for the organisation.

Conclusion

In this case study, the skills and behaviours of building relationships and man-aging stakeholders were beneficial and positive for Serena and for the organisation. Despite her lack of corporate experience, Serena demonstrated a mature and skilful application of high-integrity political astuteness, which delivered results for her and the organisation.

Case study 2: Dealing with political blockers

Organisational context

The organisation is a consumer goods company based in the UK. The individual sharing her story – Serena – joined the organisation on a six-month contract, into a team that managed sales and merchandising for large client accounts. Serena was a recent graduate at the time and saw this as an opportunity to gain experience of a workplace, explore ideas and build relationships.

Situation

Serena heard about an external initiative within her company's industry, which aimed to support women in their careers and to progress in the sector. The initiative had arranged a one-day networking event which her company was supporting. Serena learnt that some of her colleagues were attending, and she thought it would be valuable for her own learning and also offer potential networking opportunities.

Serena asked the manager leading this initiative in her company, Jane, to support her attendance to the event but Jane didn't do this, saying that Serena wasn't a permanent employee and was nearing the end of her six-month contract. Despite this setback, Serena decided to purchase a ticket independently to attend the event. She agreed to attend the event together with colleagues from a different part of her company and offered to prepare a report on learnings from the day to be shared internally after the event.

At the event, Jane was very surprised to see Serena there and asked who had invited her. Jane gave the impression that she thought Serena was 'getting above herself'. Serena was told that other people had raised the issue of why she was attending the event. Serena felt that Jane was a 'blocker' and preventing her from accessing broader development opportunities.

Serena found the event very useful and has stayed in touch with the network and spoke at a recent event of theirs. She now has a mentor from the network as well.

Observations

Jane exhibited the negative side of organisational politics whereby her actions and behaviours appear to be self-serving, eroded motivation and trust from Serena, and weren't in line with the aims of the initiative she was working on.

Serena's reflections on the case

Serena is frustrated looking back on this case, feeling that she felt some of the women involved were not open to helping other women get on, and that they wanted to be 'the one woman in the room leading this'. She experienced some of her colleagues as political blockers to other women.

Serena believes that some women were not 'taking others with them on the journey' and that Jane was exhibiting the 'Queen Bee syndrome' of not supporting other women to rise up the organisation with her.

Serena realised that she was being blocked by someone and therefore she had to build allies and form win-win authentic relationships to move forward which she did, both within her own company and across the industry initiative.

Serena also noted that in this case and in other situations she has experienced people taking on an organisational role espousing a certain aim (in this case supporting women's career growth) while in their daily work activities they act in ways which are counter to that goal (blocking women's participation in this network). This gap between the position people take up publicly and how they act in their daily lives is worth further reflection

Political learnings and outcomes

We think Serena demonstrated important strengths here:

Personal attitude and commitment – Serena was keen to attend this event and worked to show colleagues that she didn't just want a day out, but was ready to report back on the event for others.

Authenticity – being open about her intentions and explaining what she was looking for and why it was important to her.

Stakeholder analysis – understanding the intentions and styles of those around her enabled Serena to take sensible steps forward to reach her goals.

Negative politics – being aware of how people can use informal power for negative aims was helpful for Serena in this case.

Trying different methods – Serena tried and failed to bond with the person who was leading the initiative in her company, and then consciously thought, 'what else can I do here?' Her proactive way of trying different approaches paid off for her in this situation.

Conclusion

Although this case contains some disappointing negative examples of organisational politics, it also shows how someone was able to manage that situation effectively. With a strong will and the confidence to continue to engage and build allies where possible, Serena was able to come through the situation with her integrity and authenticity intact and was able to continue to build an effective network with others in her industry.

Case study 3: Managing perceptions

This case illustrates the costs of not engaging in the politics of reputation management. The client was a senior executive, who – in contrast to some of her colleagues – appeared to have the experience and maturity to understand the organisational system, the 'way things are done' and how to leverage internal networks. Heather had observed various levels of organisational politics and felt that she displayed political behaviours in a direct and transparent way. Other colleagues did not show the same level of transparency.

The organisation is a professional services firm, with a global footprint. This specific scenario is based in a country with high levels of corruption, issues with following legislation and guidance. The client was a Black female, who saw herself as having a firm, direct and clear management style. She viewed her style as being:

- based on high standards and setting such expectations with her team
- clear and concise about complex work to enable problem-solving and completion of work on time and to the standard required
- rigorous and applying high levels of care and attention to quality of work.

She was therefore shocked when a number of complaints were raised about her management style by a long-term member of her team.

The colleague managed internal organisational politics adroitly. He had built a strong personal network that he managed closely. The motivation of the complainant was unclear, but the coach suspected that the colleague saw an opportunity to replace someone he saw as politically vulnerable.

Rather than change her management style or fight back, the client requested a change of role to another country location. This was granted. The client discussed the situation in detail with her coach. They both concluded that:

- Perceptions vs. reality had impacted significantly on Heather in terms of how she was viewed by others. These views were based on second-hand and anecdotal knowledge rather than first-hand interaction to assess behaviours.
- Individual values were the key factor in driving behaviours for both parties. This situation demonstrated the negative side of organisational politics, whereby the colleague's behaviours were wholly focused on achieving personal goals at the expense of others.
- She valued achieving a high quality of work on time and to a certain standard. This had supported her progress so far, particularly as a Black female. Being frank, candid and direct ensured that instructions were clear and simple to understand and follow. However, this style can be problematic in cultures where greater emphasis is placed on inference than on clarity – it can be seen as bullying.
- She realised that she needed to pay much more attention to the broader team dynamics, pain points, individual concerns and development needs.

Lessons from this case include the need for greater cultural awareness and to recognise the messiness of organisational politics. By avoiding engaging with the team systems, the client eased the path for an opportunistic direct report to undermine her. The probability is high that aspects of race and gender also played a role. Clarity of the work tasks needed to be balanced by clarity around motivations and experience in the workplace.

For coaches, it's important to help clients step back from their task role and view the team and the client's role within it from an external perspective. Had the client built her own support network, she would have been far less vulnerable and the colleague more cautious about challenging her. In this case, it was too late to do either of these – so, the role of the coach is to ensure that clients address these issues before the knives are out!

Case study 4: Nurturing collaborative working

This case demonstrates how engaging with politics is likely to have achieved the preferred outcome for the client. The client who is one of the founders of a start-up unconsciously assumes that individuals within the organisation will automatically comply with his wishes for a change in working practices, without being aware that taking a political approach would facilitate agreement.

The organisation provides professional services, is based in Europe and has three founders with a range of specialisms. Their ambition is to become a leading provider by having talented team members, anticipated to attract further talent to work in and develop the organisation. This team on contractor terms are assigned projects as needed to provide the business services.

The founders know each other well and have a strong, positive working relationship, which allows for open and honest conversations. As is usual with start-up organisations, the founders deliver essential organisational activities. Not all are willing to be involved with the 3 hours of essential training scheduled at regular intervals. This fixed mode of delivery means that individual learning styles aren't considered to lead to repetition of material, lost time and disengagement with the training material. Without resolving this situation, the preferred solution is to delegate the training to the wider team, releasing time for the founders to focus on strategy and client partnerships.

Although the client sees the value of delegation in giving and encouraging colleagues to take responsibility for development opportunities, he hasn't considered the best way to implement and gain agreement. He is also uncomfortable with raising this suggestion with his co-founders, leaving him frustrated and resentful.

The culture of the organisation is indicative of the location where organisational politics developed and deployed through cultivating the necessary interpersonal skills aren't openly recognised as a way of facilitating acceptance of changes to working practices. This means that challenging decisions are probably seen as best avoided, resulting in disengagement, lack of commitment and the frustration displayed by the client.

The way forward is for the coach to help the client to recognise that a different approach is needed to encourage engagement from the team, being both the co-founders and the contracted colleagues. As organisations mature, it's necessary to deploy functions to release leaders to work 'on' rather than 'in' the business. Being political means offering comprehensive communication of the reasons for delegating activities and informed by the benefits anticipated for both the personnel and the development of the organisation. In this scenario, inviting the contracted colleagues into a dialogue about good practice in delivering the training helps to motivate and demonstrate the actions of a caring employer and encourages collaborative working, all attributes of effective leadership.

Appendix 4: Illustrations and charts from research

Table A1 Survey response to the question, 'What is your own view of politics within an organisation?'

Audience: Leaders, Coaches and Mentors, and Supervisors

Answer Choices	Leaders		Coaches/Mentors		Supervisors	
	Percentage	No. of responses	Percentage	No. of responses	Percentage	No. of responses
Neither a good nor bad thing*	57.76	67	80.30	106	80.85	38
To be avoided at all costs	25.00	29	11.36	15	8.51	4
A necessary evil	16.38	19	7.58	10	4.26	2
By and large positive	0.86	1	0.76	1	6.38	3
Something I don't notice	0.00	0	0.00	0	0.00	0
Total	**100%**	**116**	**100%**	**132**	**100%**	**47**

*It all depends on the motivation and how it is put into practice.

Table A2 Survey response to the question, 'What is your view of the importance of executives having "political astuteness" (being politically aware and able to work with different power relationships and conflicting objectives)?'

Audience: Leaders, Coaches and Mentors, and Supervisors

Answer Choices	Leaders		Coaches/Mentors		Supervisors	
	Percentage	No. of responses	Percentage	No. of responses	Percentage	No. of responses
Very important	55.17	64	77.28	102	82.97	39
Quite important	34.48	40	18.18	24	12.77	6
Somewhat important	5.17	6	2.27	3	2.13	1
To be avoided	3.46	4	2.27	3	2.13	1
Unimportant	1.72	2	0.00	0	0.00	0
Total	**100%**	**116**	**100%**	**132**	**100%**	**47**

Figure A1 Survey response to the question, 'What are some of the most negative impacts on people and the organisation of politics in organisations?'
Audience: Leaders, Coaches and Mentors, and Supervisors

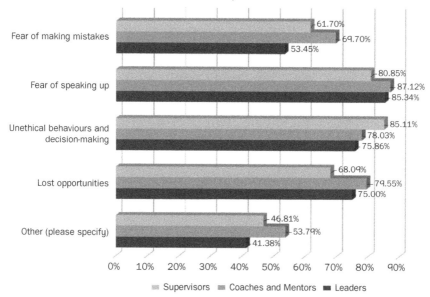

Figure A2 Survey response to the question, 'What are some of the most positive impacts on people and the organisation of being politically competent?'
Audience: Leaders, Coaches and Mentors and Supervisors

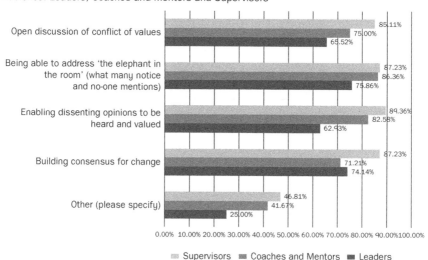

Figure A3 Survey response to the question, 'How often do you encounter politics as an issue in your role as a leader?'

Audience: Leaders

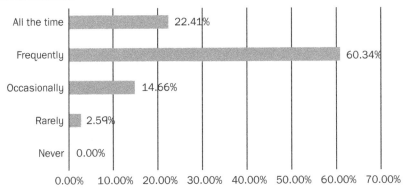

Figure A4 Survey response to the question, 'How conscious are you of your personal biases about politics (positive or negative) influencing your role as a leader?'

Audience: Leaders

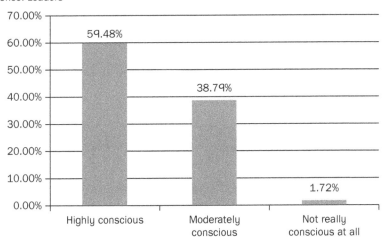

Figure A5 Survey response to the question, 'What in your opinion are the biggest challenges for leaders in managing organisational politics?'

Audience: Leaders

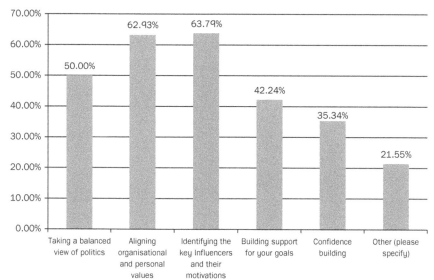

Figure A6 Survey response to the question, 'How often do you encounter politics as an issue in your coaching assignments?'

Audience: Coaches and Mentors

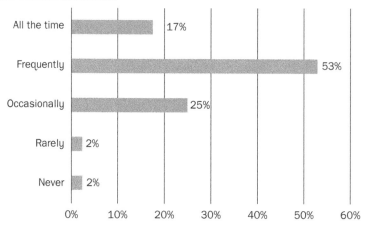

Figure A7 Survey response to the question, 'How conscious are you of your personal biases about politics (positive or negative) influencing your work with clients?'
Audience: Coaches and Mentors

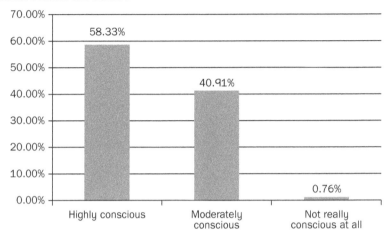

Figure A8 Survey response to the question, 'What in your view are the challenges for clients in managing organisational politics?'
Audience: Coaches and Mentors

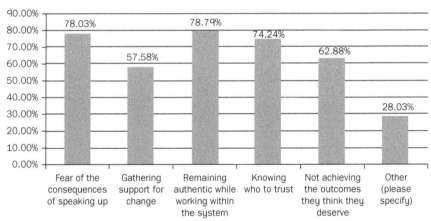

Figure A9 Survey response to the question 'What in your opinion is the most effective way in which coaches support clients through organisational politics?'

Audience: Coaches and Mentors

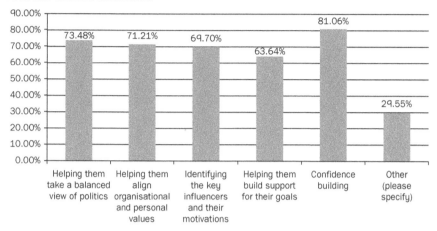

Figure A10 Survey response to the question, 'What is the impact on you when clients bring issues with political dimensions?'

Audience: Coaches and Mentors

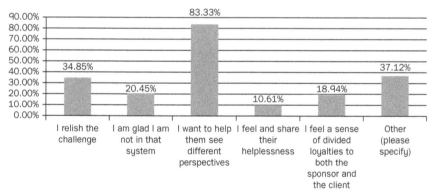

Table A3 Survey response to the question, 'What do you help your clients with when recognising and understanding political dimensions?'

Audience: Coaches and Mentors

Answer Choices	Responses	
	Percentage	Number
I help them recognise that there is a political dimension to an issue they bring	74.24	98
I help them understand the political dynamics of an issue	77.27	102
I help them identify the choices they have	90.15	119
I help them establish the values they want to apply to those choices	78.03	103
I help them to be authentic in their responses to political issues	82.55	109
Other (please specify)	25.00	33
	Answered	**132**

Figure A11 Survey response to the question, 'How often do you encounter politics as an issue in your coaching supervision?'

Audience: Supervisors

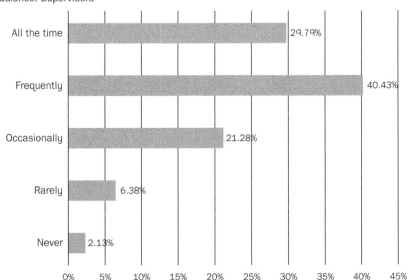

Figure A12 Survey response to the question, 'How conscious are you of your personal biases about politics (positive or negative) influencing your work with coaches?"
Audience: Supervisors

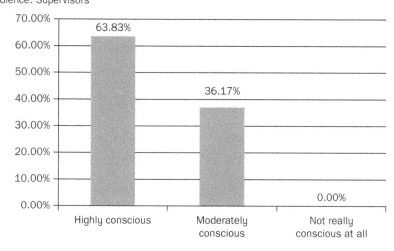

Figure A13 Survey response to the question, 'What in your opinion is the most effective way in which coaches support clients through organisational politics?'
Audience: Supervisors

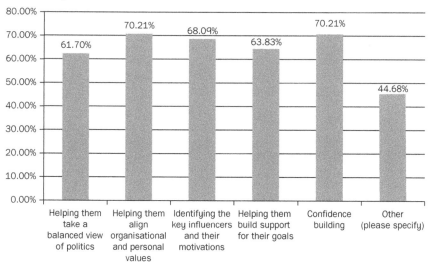

Table A4 Survey response to the question, 'What do you help your clients with when recognising and understanding political dimensions?'

Audience: Supervisors

Answer Choices	Responses	
	Percentage	Number
I help them recognise that there is a political dimension to an issue they bring	76.60	36
I help them understand the political dynamics of an issue	85.11	40
I help them identify the choices they have	72.34	34
I help them establish the values they want to apply to those choices	76.60	36
I help them to be authentic in their responses to political issues	74.47	35
Other (please specify)	48.94	23
	Answered	**47**

Index

Page numbers in italics are figures; with 't' are tables.